The What *to* Expect

Babysitter and Nanny Handbook

HEIDI MURKOFF
WITH SHARON MAZEL

POCKET
BOOKS

LONDON . NEW YORK . SYDNEY . TORONTO . DUBLIN

649

7

This edition published by Pocket Books, 2004
An imprint of Simon & Schuster UK Ltd
A Viacom company

Copyright © What to Expect LLC, 2003
Interior illustrations copyright © Judy Francis, 2003

1   3   5   7   9   10   8   6   4   2

Simon & Schuster UK Ltd
Africa House
64–78 Kingsway
London WC2B 6AH

www.simonsays.co.uk

Simon & Schuster Australia
Sydney

A CIP catalogue record for this book is available from the British Library

ISBN 1-4165-0211-4
EAN 9781416502111

Printed and bound in Great Britain by
Cox & Wyman, Reading, Berkshire

Contents

Contents

a word to parents

Leaving your child with someone else can be a little tough. Make that a *lot* tough. Even if you've selected the best childcare provider you could find (and you took your time looking). Even if she comes with flawless references (from parents who wish only that their children were still young enough to need a childminder). Even if she has years of experience (and it shows the first time she picks up your baby, who stops crying instantly). Even if she's Mary Poppins herself (with the perfect mixture of silliness and no-nonsense firmness that keeps kids happy *and* well behaved – plus the charming habit of occasionally breaking into song).

That's where *The What to Expect® Babysitter and Nanny Handbook* comes in. There's something here for everyone – from the seasoned pro to the newest childcarer on the block, from the live-in nanny to the Saturday night babysitter: what to do in an emergency. How to handle a play session with playmates. Plus tips on feeding, sleeping and bathing. It's all in these pages – advice that you and your childcare provider can trust, from the *What to Expect* team.

Though this book is geared to your childminder (just as the *What to Expect®* parenting books are geared to you), don't pass it along without taking a peek. Throughout are answers to the questions that childcarers ask most – often questions that

what's inside

Leaving your child with someone else is one of life's greatest leaps of faith. That's why you should look (and check references) before you make that leap, and then make sure that your care provider has all the information she needs to best care for your child or children (in a form she'll want to read). And you'll want that information to be not just the most up-to-date, but also specifically geared to *your* child or children. It's all inside these pages.

will give you valuable insight into your care provider's mind (and what her day-to-day life with your child is really like). Communication questions (about touchy topics, such as asking for a raise or the expense reimbursement you keep forgetting about). Questions about child-rearing philosophies (what if she's a fan of schedules and you're not?). Questions about on-the-job expectations (you like a clean house on your return from work, a goal she finds hard to meet, considering the mess your hurricane twins leave in their path). And, because no one's advice is more important than yours, there's an entire fill-in-the-blanks section in the back of the book dedicated to the unique needs of your unique family. Here's where you can jot down (in pencil, so you can erase and adjust as your child grows) everything about your child that you'd like your care provider to know – from bedtime rituals to TV rules. Armed with these notes and the information you provide on the Emergency Information pages inside the front and back covers of this book, your baby-sitter will be able to personalize the care she gives – and you'll be able to breathe easier while you're away from home.

Wishing you the happiest of childcare experiences.

◆ ◆ ◆

a word to the childcarer

HELP WANTED

Childcarer needed: Storyteller, pooper-scooper, entertainer (ability to make funny faces a plus), short-order cook (experience with peanut butter and jelly preferred), floor pacer (must be able to walk and comfort fussy baby at the same time). Should have strong shoulders (for a baby to cuddle against and a toddler to cry on), a soft heart (and a soft spot for children of all ages), a good sense of humour (it will come in handy) and nerves of steel (they will, too). Needed for peace negotiations (separating fighting preschoolers), security issues (keeping those precious bundles safe), transportation (to and from the playground) and possible health-care emergencies (boo-boos big and small).

Childcare Notes

Okay, so this might not have been the ad you answered for your childcare job, but let's face it, it might as well have been. Being a nanny, baby-sitter or care provider of any kind means you do all of the above – and much, much more. From dispensing love to dispensing discipline, from pushing a pushchair to pushing a swing, from warming bottles to warming baths, from scrubbing dirty chins to scrubbing marker off the living room wall, there's a whole lot more to caring for a child than any newspaper ad could possibly list. Like most other jobs, childcare has its ups (those special, sticky-fingered hugs meant just for you) and its downs (those days when the baby won't take 'nap' for an answer). It has rewards beyond what comes in a paycheque, and frustrations that can sometimes make you wonder whether the paycheque is worth it. But on good days and bad, caring for a child is a job that makes a difference.

USING THE HANDBOOK

This book is designed to make that job easier (though there's never anything *easy* about caring for children). It starts with a list of parent contact information and emergency numbers on the inside covers, then the pages that follow contain tips, advice and other information about all your childcare concerns, as well as commonsense answers to the questions childminders ask most often. Covering everything from the basics (like changing a nappy and winding a baby) to thesituations that can challenge even the most experienced caregiver (how *do* you discipline a preschooler?), from the essentials of safety and health (complete with a step-by-step first-aid section) to the business end of the job (how to communicate with the parents), *The What to Expect® Babysitter and Nanny Handbook* is the essential guide for all childcarers.

What's more, the book has been personalized just for you.

Flip to the back, and you'll find information and instructions specifically about the child or children in your care. As you know, every child – and every family – is unique. Each child has a different personality and different needs; each family has different rules and different philosophies. Make sure the parents have written down what *they* think is important for you to know. These guidelines will give you the inside scoop on everything from favourite games to favourite bedtime stories; from comfort techniques that work like a charm to bedtime routines that weave sleepy magic. Plus, you'll find all the house rules on TV watching, between-meal snacking, after-school play sessions – you name it.

In the end, how you make use of *The What to Expect® Babysitter and Nanny Handbook* is up to you. If you're a first-timer, or if it's been a while since your last childcare job, you may want to read it cover to cover. If you're a seasoned pro, you're likely to find the fill-in pages the most helpful section, although you still might want to read through the book for some new insights and tricks of the trade.

Either way, welcome to this book – and to the wonderful world of childcare!

◆ ◆ ◆

For emergency numbers and contact information, see the inside front and back covers of this book.

◆ ◆ ◆

For essential information on first aid, CPR and emergency response, see Chapter 11.

◆ ◆ ◆

CHAPTER 1

the parent connection

Sure, you may be the one who's changing the nappies, filling the bottles, fixing the snacks and supervising the naps each day. But you're not in it alone (even if it sometimes seems that way). Caring for a child doesn't just mean you're part of a family – it means you're part of a team. To ensure the best care for a child, you'll need to work closely with those other most important team members, the parents, giving, taking, sharing, communicating and connecting with them.

Childcare Notes

making the connection

COMMUNICATION

Working with the parents to provide the best care for their child will also make your relationship with them a winning one. And since every good relationship depends on talking openly and honestly, keep these keys to effective parent–childcarer communication in mind:

PLAN AHEAD. There are plenty of how-to's in this book, but the most important ones start on page 212. These specific instructions from the parents will tell you exactly how to tailor the care you're giving to fit the child you're giving it to. Does the child need to nap during the day? Should the baby be fed on demand or when the clock says it's time? Can the toddler watch TV? Is the computer off-limits? How long can the preschooler play on the computer? What foods should the child eat – or not eat? What about snacks? How are tantrums handled? When a child misbehaves, what should you do? What about dummies? How about bottles?

KEEP A DAILY LOG. There will be days when the baby won't stop crying, or the toddler is in high-energy mode or the Reception-age child has back-to-back activities. And those will be the days when you'll forget what time the baby ate last, or how long the toddler napped, or what the Reception-age child had for a snack. The best way to remember the kind of information parents will want at day's end is to keep a daily log as you go. Not only won't you forget the important details, but you won't have to try to give parents a blow-by-blow when they arrive home (to a child who's screaming for their attention). See pages 16–17 for a sample daily log.

DEBRIEF AT DAY'S END. A daily log is invaluable, but it shouldn't take the place of daily conversation. The log will cover how much cereal the baby ate or what time the preschooler downed his medicine – but not the shaky first pre-steps the one-year-old took or the adorable thing the two-year-old said on the way to the park.

MEET REGULARLY. Daily recaps can be rushed and a little stressful. The parents will likely want to meet regularly with you (perhaps once a week, or every other week, or just once a month) to discuss any issues that may need some extra time and attention. These meetings can take place in person or over the telephone. Think of these 'relationship checkups' as your chance to air your concerns, opinions and problems, as well as to give positive feedback (such as how much you enjoy caring for the children) to the parents.

FINDING TIME FOR A DAILY LOG

Q *'The parents have asked me to keep a daily log, but between caring for three kids and doing light cleaning, I can't seem to find the time to jot stuff down. What should I do?'*

A The purpose of a daily log is to communicate with the parents, and that's what you need to do right now. Talk to the parents and let them know that you have too little time during the day to write things down. Suggest that you'll write down only the most essential information, but you'll stay a few minutes later to give a more in-depth rundown of the day's events if they want. Or ask the parents if you can call or e-mail them during the day to update them on late-breaking news, such as baby's first step or a five-year-old's successfully tied shoe.

did you know?

While the most important part of your work is providing care for a little one (or little ones), your employers might also expect you to do a few extras. To avoid trouble later, ask ahead so you'll know whether they'll want you to handle additional chores, such as doing laundry (the child's or the entire family's?), cooking, cleaning, running errands, and so on.

END-OF-THE-DAY MESS

Q *'The parents have made it clear to me that they want to come home to a clean house. I understand that this is important to them, but some days getting the house spotless before they arrive is just unrealistic.'*

A Life with small children is by nature messy – every parent knows that. Still, everybody's happier when the house is put back together at the end of the day. The best plan is to try to clean as you go, rather than letting the dishes, laundry and toys pile up all day. And unless you're caring for a baby, there's no need to go it alone in the housekeeping department. Even toddlers are old enough to enlist in cleanups – and all children are more likely to pitch in if you make the job a game (see page 90).

On the other hand, if you feel the parents' expectations aren't quite fair, talk the realities over with them at a meeting.

ASKING FOR A RAISE

Q *'I've been childminding for one family for well over a year now, and I was hoping they would give me a raise. How can I ask them for more money?'*

A Come to the bargaining table prepared. First find out what other families in your area are paying their nannies. Make sure you compare your salary with those of nannies whose qualifications and experience are similar to yours. Come armed with an amount that would work for you, and don't be afraid to say it. Then detail the reasons you deserve those extra pounds. Tell the parents how committed you are to your job and describe in detail all the ways that you have enriched – and hope to continue enriching – their children's lives. Be ready to address any issues the parents might have.

But also come prepared to be understanding and flexible. If the parents can't afford to increase your pay, perhaps they can offer you a little more vacation time. Or work with them to come up with some other (more affordable) way they can show their appreciation, such as a bonus.

MAKE OFF-HOURS OFF-LIMITS

Q *'I work as a live-in nanny. I'm off on weekends, but I don't always go away. Sometimes I feel as if the kids (and parents) expect me to be there for them even during my off-hours. How do I tell them this isn't fair?'*

A Let the parents know that while you enjoy being part of the family, you also enjoy your time off from the family. Tell them (nicely) that having your Saturday morning sleep-in interrupted by a couple of kids jumping on your bed isn't exactly your idea of fun (or your idea of time off). Explain that you need your weekend R&R so that you'll feel refreshed for another week come Monday morning. Remind the children (again, nicely) that just because you're around on the weekends doesn't mean you're on duty – but that you'll be available to play with them when the workweek begins again.

MAKE YOURSELF AT HOME ... WITHIN REASON

W hile it's important to fit in with the family you're working for, it's also important to remember that you're an employee. Make sure you and the parents have gone over the house ground rules, then keep the following tips in mind – even if you're just baby-sitting for a few hours in the evening.

KEEP THE PHONE FREE. Tying up the phone line by chatting with your friends is a bad idea. Not only does it mean you're not paying attention to the children, but it also means the line won't be available for incoming calls from the parents and others. Make any necessary phone calls (to your doctor, for instance, or to check up on your own children) at naptime – and then keep it short.

KEEP YOUR MOBILE PHONE FREE. So, if you can't tie up the family phone, there's nothing wrong with talking up a storm on your mobile phone – right? Wrong. Again, there's the attention issue. Keep the mobile handy in case of emergency, or to contact the parents (or be contacted by them) while you're out with the child, but don't use it for catching up with friends during work hours. (If you end up using your own mobile a lot for communicating with the parents, you can ask them to pay for part of the monthly bill. Or maybe they have a mobile phone you can use on duty.)

USE THE COMPUTER *only* if the parents ask you to e-mail and instant-message them during the day. Don't put it to personal use unless they've said you can, and then use it only when the child is napping (and don't make the mistake of visiting Web sites that the parents wouldn't approve of).

DON'T INVITE GUESTS OVER. The only guests you should be hosting on the job are playmates of the child (and their parents or caregivers), unless you've been told otherwise.

DON'T BE A LARDER RAIDER. Most parents will be happy to provide you with meals and snacks while you're on the job – and will probably tell you to help yourself to anything you want. But don't consider this an invitation to eat them out of house and home. Be polite in the larder – don't eat the whole box of biscuits, or drink the last sip of the orange juice, or polish off the leftovers they were saving for dinner.

JOINING THE FAMILY VACATION

Q *'The parents have told me they'd like me to come along – and work – on their family vacation. I'm excited about travelling, but unsure of what my duties will be.'*

A Sometimes the perks of the job (travelling to exotic locations) are balanced by the somewhat less exciting aspects (sleeping in the same room as the kids, limiting the

don't let them leave home without telling you . . .

SAFE AND SOUND

Parents will provide specific instructions and an emergency contact list before they go out. Don't let them leave home without showing you where the list is posted. Or turn to the front of this book for a copy of the list.

privacy, please

Whether you're a live-in nanny or a part-time baby-sitter, you'll need to respect the privacy of the family you work for.

■ **DON'T SNOOP.** It might be hard not to read a letter left open on the counter. But don't give in to temptation.

■ **GIVE THE FAMILY SPACE.** When the parents are having a discussion between themselves, leave the room quietly.

■ **NEVER TELL.** Anything that happens within a family's four walls should stay there. Don't gossip with anyone about what goes on behind closed doors.

margaritas to nights off). But as long as you know what to expect (and what will be expected of you) before you pack that suitcase, the family trip should be a pleasant break for everyone. Be sure you work out all the details ahead of time with the parents. Will you have to care for the children round the clock, or will you have at least some nights off? Will you be expected to work seven days a week (if the trip lasts a week or longer), or will you continue to get weekends off? Will you be paid overtime if you work longer hours than you do at home? And will the parents cover all your travel expenses – or just airfare, hotel and meals when you're on duty? The most important

thing to keep in mind when you're a nanny-to-go: Even if the locale you're visiting is a hot spot for vacationers, this isn't your vacation.

NOT ENOUGH PRIVACY

Q *'As a live-in nanny, I find that I don't have enough privacy. For example, the kids are always popping into my room without knocking.'*

A Privacy is definitely a two-way street – which means you're also entitled to it. Be sure to set ground rules that will help to ensure your privacy (as the parents have likely set ground rules to ensure theirs). For instance, children should be taught that your room is open to them by invitation only (and then only after they've knocked). A sign on your door (with a green side for knock and come in, and a red side for privacy) may help the kids understand this. A small fridge in your room might be a nice touch – so you won't have to wrap yourself up in a robe and parade through the kitchen every time you need a cold drink – as well as a phone of your own so you can have conversations without an audience.

NANNY-CAM ANXIETY

Q *'The parents I work for have put in a "nanny cam". They didn't tell me about it, but I've seen it. I'm uncomfortable – not because I'm afraid they'll see me do something wrong, but because I wish I could talk to them about it. Should I bring the subject up?'*

A More and more parents are choosing to place nanny cams around the house. Some will tell you up front that they'll be videotaping; others may do it on the sly.

If the nanny cam makes you uncomfortable, it's best not to keep your feelings to yourself. Bring it up at your next meeting (not at the beginning or end of the day, when conversation is rushed). Tell the parents that you'd be more than happy to address any trust issues, but you'd prefer to do it through open, honest communication. If you feel the nanny cam violates your privacy, speak up about that, too; although the parents may have the right to videotape you, you have the right to express your concerns about being watched.

PLAYING THE PARENT

Q *'The parents I work for are out of the house all day. I'm with their two little girls more than they are, and sometimes I feel as if I'm in a better position to know what's best for the children. Should I say something?'*

A When you're spending so much time with children, it's hard not to start feeling that you know best – or at least more than the parents do. And there may be times when you do know better. But there's a fine line between parenting and caregiving – and it's a line that a nanny shouldn't cross. Though you may occasionally bring up (always gently) a few issues that concern you the most (and that most directly relate to you, like a toddler being overscheduled or a

conflict resolution checklist

Hopefully, your relationship with the child's parents will be mostly smooth sailing, but face facts: conflicts will come up. When something goes wrong, here's how to bring the problem out in the open:

DO

☑ **DO BE HONEST.** Without honest communication, little misunderstandings become big ones. Talk openly about what's upsetting you — and you can expect the parents to do the same.

☑ **DO BE SPECIFIC.** Instead of complaining in general ('The day is so stressful'), use examples that make your case clearly ('There's no time in between driving to activities for me to get the laundry done').

☑ **DO WORK ON A RESOLUTION.** Together, try to find a solution to the problem — not only for the child's sake, but to ensure continued success of the relationship.

☑ **DO KEEP THE CHILD OUT OF IT.** Issues or disagreements about the child or the job should *never* be discussed with or in front of the child. You might be working *with* the child, but you're working *for* the parents.

DON'T

☒ **DON'T BOTTLE IT UP.** Instead of letting all your complaints pile up for months, then spitting them out in a resentful tirade, focus on one major issue at a time.

☒ **DON'T ACCUSE.** Avoid putting the parents on the defensive. Instead of saying, 'You keep doing this', say, 'I'm not happy when this happens.' It also helps to put a positive spin on it: 'I think it might work better if . . .'

☒ **DON'T IGNORE THE RESPONSE.** Remember, there are two sides to every issue. Even if you don't agree with the parents' side, it's important that you listen to it.

☒ **DON'T TAKE IT PERSONALLY.** Parents want what's best for their children — and when they ask you to change the way you do something, that's the reason. Try not to see suggestions as a criticism of you.

preschooler refusing to clean up because the parents never expect him to), always keep in mind who's the boss.

Remember, too, that putting a positive spin on your 'issue' will make it a lot easier for the parents to hear you. Refer to the tips on page 9.

ON-THE-SPOT DECISIONS

Q *'Often I'm in situations in which I need to make a decision about something the parents and I haven't discussed. For example, the child I care for was playing at a friend's house and the other child's parent offered to drive her home. But I don't know if my employer wants the child to get a lift with other parents. What should I do?'*

A Hopefully, the parents have given you the authority to make decisions within set guidelines – such as how to dress the child or what to give her for lunch. But when you don't have the go-ahead for a major issue like this one, don't go ahead without it. If you can't reach the parents by phone, stick with what you know is okay until you have time to talk the matter over with them.

SHARING DIFFERENCES

Your cultural background may be different from that of the family you work for. Or the family may practise a different religion – or have different customs – from the ones you're used to. They might even have an altogether different outlook on life. But don't think of these differences as problems; instead, see them as a way to expand your horizons.

RESPECT THE FAMILY'S CUSTOMS. Never make fun of their heritage or try to teach the child that your way is better.

LEARN BY ASKING. A good carer becomes part of the family, whether she's living in or working nine to five. And that means learning as much about them as possible. Don't be afraid to ask questions that will help you appreciate the family's culture and customs.

SHARE YOUR OWN CULTURE. A different worldview can expand anyone's horizons. If the family is open to the idea, teach the child (and parents) about your culture. Explaining how holidays are celebrated in your family, singing native songs or baking recipes you grew up with lets a family learn more about you, while enriching a child's life. It can also bring all of you closer together.

RELIGIOUS DIFFERENCES

Q *'I'm Christian and the family I work for is Jewish. My own children love it when I read them stories from our Bible. Is it okay for me to read these stories to the children I baby-sit for if they're all from the Old Testament?'*

A As you know, religion is a deeply personal issue. Even people of the same religion often take very different spiritual paths. So before you show your Bible book to the children in your care, you'll need to pass it by their parents to see if they're comfortable with it. If they're not, perhaps they have their own Bible book they'd like you to share with the children instead. Or maybe they'd prefer that you stay away from religion altogether and stick to other storybooks (more *Cat in the Hat*, less *David and Goliath*). As with any decision they make, remember to respect it.

HAPPIER HOMECOMINGS

After a full day away, parents look forward to nothing more than holding that little bundle of joy they've missed all day. So the last thing they'll want is for that little bundle to be screaming, dirty, tired or unfed. For happier homecomings, try to take care of the basics before that key turns in the lock.

FEEDING. How you deal with end-of-the-day feeding will depend on what the child is eating:

■ If the baby is drinking only formula, ask Mum and Dad if they want to give the afternoon or evening bottle when they return or if they'd prefer to come home to a happily fed baby. If they want to do the afternoon feeding, prepare a bottle for them.

- If Mum is breast-feeding, she may be eager to nurse the moment she walks in the door. Or she may want some time to unwind before putting baby to breast. Her preferences will determine when you should last feed the baby.

- If the parents will be having dinner with a toddler or an older child, be sure to give him a snack (so he isn't too hungry to wait). But don't give it so late in the day that it ruins his appetite for dinner.

SLEEPING. Most parents will want some 'baby time' when they arrive home – so try to plan the child's nap so that she will be awake on their return. On the other hand, most parents will also appreciate some grown-up time during their evening, which means that the last nap can't be too close to bedtime. Talk the sleeping schedule out with the parents.

CLEANING UP. A sweet-smelling baby is what Mum and Dad have been picturing all day, so make sure that the baby greeting them at the door is in a clean nappy (no smelly poo, please) and clean outfit, with hands washed (no dirt under the fingernails from the playground) and face wiped clean (so there are no tell-tale signs of the sweet potatoes he ate for lunch).

PREPARING. Do an inventory before the parents arrive. All the nappies used up? Running low on formula? Out of the child's favourite snack bars? Speak up and alert the parents.

Remember, too, to clean the pushchair, nappy bag and carrier before you go. Throw away old bottles of formula, crumpled tissues and soiled nappies. Tidy up the toys and put dirty clothing in the hamper.

OVERTIME

Q *'The parents are always coming home 15 minutes late – which cuts into my evening with my own kids. They also don't offer me overtime. Should I say something?'*

A Sometimes even the best-intentioned parents are so busy worrying about their own schedules that they forget their childcarers have schedules, too. It's time for a gentle but firm reminder at the next meeting (call one soon if there isn't one on the books for several weeks). Explain that you understand (all too well!) how hard it is to balance family and work – and that you don't mind if they return home a few minutes late now and then because of an unexpected traffic jam or a meeting that ran over. But also explain that because you have family commitments of your own, you'd like them to keep to the arranged schedule as much as possible. And that when they can't keep to it, you'd appreciate a call in advance (if possible). Another item that needs to be on the agenda is fair compensation for those late nights, whether it's extra pay or being able to leave early (or come in late) once in a while. But don't be too hard on the parents (especially since you've been there and done that yourself); try to be somewhat flexible in your own schedule.

GIVING NOTICE

Q *'I've decided to go back to college, and I'm not sure how to tell the parents I'm leaving.'*

A Most parents would rather lose a big business deal than a valued nanny (who, for a busy family, is just about priceless). So be gentle and thoughtful in breaking your news. First, hold a meeting to tell the parents you're leaving and why (they'll be glad to know it isn't something they did). Saying it in a letter may be easier on you, but lacks that personal touch they'd probably appreciate. Next, give as much advance notice as possible (*never* less than two weeks), and set a date to leave. You may want to offer to help interview or train a new caregiver (nobody knows the ropes better than someone who has climbed them herself). Finally, ask for a letter of recommendation. Even if you're not planning to take another job right away, a letter from your employers (assuming they'll say nice things about you) may come in handy down the road.

NOTABLE NOTES

What's the child been up to all day? Parents will want to know every little detail you can remember, and probably a few you'll forget – if you don't write them down. Be sure to have the answers to the questions below (preferably written down; see pages 16–17 for a sample daily log) when the parents walk in the front door.

☑ NEWBORN TO 6 MONTHS

❑ What did the two of you do today?

❑ Did you go outside for a walk?

❑ Was the baby fussy?

❑ How many ounces of formula or breast milk did the baby drink?

❑ How often did he eat?

❑ When was he last fed – and is he hungry now?

❑ How many nappies did you go through today?

❑ When was the baby last changed? Is he wet now?

❑ How much did he nap?

❑ Do we have enough formula/nappies/wipes or other supplies to make it through the night? Are we low on anything?

❑ Do we have enough breast milk for tomorrow?

❑ Were there any problems we should know about?

❑ Do you have any great baby stories to share?

☑ 6 TO 12 MONTHS

❑ What did the two of you do today?

❑ Did you go outside for a walk?

❑ What did the baby eat? When? How much did she eat?

❑ How much did she drink?

❑ How much did she nap?

❑ Did she master any new tricks today?

❑ Were there any problems we should know about?

❑ Any great stories to share?

☑ TODDLER

❑ What did the two of you do today?

❏ Did you go outside for a walk? To the playground?

❏ What did the child eat and drink?

❏ When was his last meal or snack?

❏ Did he play with any friends? Go to playgroup? How did it go?

❏ What did he do at preschool?

❏ Are there any notes from his preschool teachers?

❏ Did he nap? How much?

❏ How did he behave today?

❏ Did he accomplish anything new (use the potty, clean up nicely, and so on)?

❏ Did he watch TV today? How much?

❏ What games did he play? What books did you read together?

❏ Were there any problems we should know about?

❏ Any great stories to share?

☑ 4 TO 6 YEARS

❏ What did the two of you do today?

❏ Did you go outside for a walk? Play ball? Bicycle ride? Go to the playground?

❏ What did the child eat and drink?

❏ When was her last meal or snack?

❏ What did she do at school today?

❏ Are there any notes from her school teachers?

❏ Did she play with any friends today? How did it go?

❏ How did she behave today?

❏ Did she use the computer today? Which games did she play? For how long?

❏ What other games did she play? What books did you read together?

❏ Did she watch TV today? Which shows? For how long?

❏ Did she have any toileting accidents?

❏ Were there any problems we should know about?

❏ Any great stories to share?

sample daily log

Use this log as the basis for one you and the parents agree on. (Perhaps you or the parents can type it up and print out a bunch of copies.) Keep one log for each child in your care and have it ready when the parents come home.

. . . .

Today's date _____ **Name of child** _____

Eating

Breakfast (time eaten, amounts and types of food) _____

_____

Lunch (time eaten, amounts and types of food) _____

_____

Dinner (time eaten, amounts and types of food) _____

_____

Snacks (time eaten, amounts and types of food) _____

_____

Comments: _____

_____

Sleeping

Napped from _____ to _____

Comments: _____

Nappies/potty

Changed # _____ nappies

Bowel movements # _____ ❑ normal ❑ loose ❑ runny

Used potty # _____

Comments: _____

_____

Bath: ❑ yes ❑ no

Medications given _____ **Times** _____ **Dosage** _____

Inside activities _____

_____

Outside activities _____

_____

Play sessions _____

_____

Preschool/school _____

_____

Child's mood: ❑ very happy ❑ happy ❑ fussy ❑ crying a lot
❑ average ❑ tired

Comments: _____

_____

Milestones and accomplishments _____

_____

_____

Cute story of the day _____

_____

_____

Problems _____

_____

Boo-boo report _____

_____

Nanny notes _____

_____

_____

_____

_____

CHAPTER 2

what to expect at every age

being a nanny is a job that comes with a million and one rewards. It's exciting to be on the front lines when a baby rolls over for the first time, to watch a one-year-old successfully stack those rings (after weeks of trying), to see a clingy preschooler make a friend at the playground. But it's also a job that comes with a million and one challenges – from figuring out how to turn off a baby's tears, to convincing a toddler to use the potty, to keeping a play session from becoming a boxing match. Knowing what to expect as a child grows will prepare you for both the rewards and the challenges that lie ahead.

newborn to 6 months

Is there anything cuter than a cuddly newborn or a roly-poly four-month-old with a toothless smile? Caring for a baby during the first six months of life presents its share of demands (and dirty nappies), but also more than its share of pleasures.

And what a jam-packed six months it will be for the baby, and for you. Jam-packed with nappy changes and bottles (and there will be plenty of those). Jam-packed with amazing growth and development. Baby will be coming a long way, baby, in the first six months – and you'll be there to provide the love, protection and stimulation that can make a lasting difference in that brand-new life.

WHAT TO EXPECT

Babies develop rapidly during the first six months, both physically and mentally. Though there can be a lot of variation among children, here's what you can generally look forward to:

- By the end of the first month, the baby should be gaining better head control and will probably be able to lift his head a bit when lying on his belly.

- By the end of the second month, start looking for baby to smile back at you. She may even begin to recognize the sound of your voice.

- Around three months, babies start to coo and babble. Strike up a conversation and watch how baby 'talks' back.

- By the end of the fourth month, baby will be squealing out loud when you get silly, so keep up the entertainment.

- Around five months, baby may begin to roll over. Once she's managed that, the days of her staying put are gone. You'll have a newly mobile baby on your hands.

■ By the end of the sixth month, many babies are sitting up. That means they've got a different view of the world and will be able to play with you in a whole new way. Time to think of some new games!

BONDING WITH BABY

Q *'I've just started caring for the most adorable two-month-old baby girl. I enjoy taking care of her, but I'm afraid I'm not bonding with her as much as I had hoped.'*

A The deep connection between caregiver and child that you're longing for doesn't develop overnight – or even in a few weeks. In fact, some of the best relationships get off to a slow start. So don't worry, and give yourself and baby time to get to know each other. It won't be long before you're the best of buds.

Keep in mind, too, that two-month-old infants, while undeniably adorable, aren't quite 'personality plus' just yet – which makes developing a relationship with them a little more challenging. In the next weeks, as the baby becomes more responsive to your advances (cooing back to your coos, smiling back to your smiles), you'll find yourself bonding plenty.

BABY BASICS

Q *'I've never cared for a newborn before, and I'm not sure how to talk to him or play with him.'*

A You may be new at the newborn thing, but you're clearly on the right track since you realize that even infants can (and should) be talked to. At this point, you don't have to worry too much about playing with the baby – just look into his eyes, hold him, coo to him, sing to him, cuddle him, laugh with him. (And while he's napping, read this book!)

did you know?

A newborn baby's head accounts for about one-quarter of his entire weight. Always support his head to keep it from flopping around.

baby safety basics

SAFE AND SOUND

Even an infant who can't yet roll over or sit up can get into a surprising amount of trouble very quickly. To protect a baby from accidents, be sure to follow *all* of these safety tips *all* the time:

■ Never smoke near the baby, whether you're in the house or outdoors.

■ Keep your eyes on him *at all times* (unless he's napping in his own home in the cot or Moses basket).

■ Keep your eyes and a hand on the baby when he's on a high surface. That means on a changing table, bed, chair or couch. Even newborns who can't roll over can suddenly stretch and fall off.

■ If there are safety straps on the changing table, use them. But don't rely on them to keep the baby secure. You still need to keep a constant eye on him – and a hand, too, if he's squirmy.

■ Never put the baby in an infant (or car) seat or carrier on a table, counter or any raised surface. A strong kick could send the seat – and baby – to the ground.

■ Never jiggle or shake the baby (even in play) or toss him up in the air. Babies can suffer permanent damage and even die from what is called shaken baby syndrome.

■ To prevent accidental strangulation, don't attach a chain or string longer than six inches to the baby's clothing, toys or other belongings. Make sure that the ends of strings in hoods, gowns and pants are knotted so that they can't slip through, and never leave cords, string, ropes or necklaces of any kind around where baby might get to them.

■ Make sure the baby's cot, playpen yard and changing table are not within reach of electric cords, telephone cords, or blind or curtain cords. All these items can strangle a baby.

■ To prevent accidental suffocation, don't leave filmy plastics, such as those used by dry cleaners, where the baby can get at them.

■ Don't leave an infant within reach of pillows, stuffed animals or other plush items.

■ Always put the baby to sleep on his back, whether it's for a short nap or at bedtime.

■ Don't let the baby sleep with pillows, comforters or stuffed toys or on a sheepskin, plush-top mattress, beanbag or waterbed. And never let the baby sleep on a bed wedged up against the wall.

■ Do not place the baby anywhere near an unguarded window, even for a second, and even if she's sound asleep.

■ Never go out, even for a moment, without the baby. It may be tempting to leave him asleep while you run to the mailbox or check the laundry in the apartment basement. Don't. A fire or an accident can happen in seconds.

■ Never leave the baby alone in a room with a pet, even a very well-behaved one.

■ Never leave the baby alone in a room with a child under five years old. A loving but over-enthusiastic bear hug could crack a rib, and even a peeka-boo game between a preschooler and an infant could result in tragic suffocation.

■ Always strap an infant into a rear-facing infant car seat or a rear-facing convertible car seat in the backseat of a car. Follow all the parents' instructions on car-seat use.

■ Never leave a child alone in a car. Even if you just have to run into the dry cleaner's, take him with you. Being left alone in a car in warm weather is especially dangerous.

6 to 12 months

During the next six months, your role as a care provider changes from chief bottle feeder and burper to sports coach (as baby learns to crawl, then walk), language tutor (as baby learns to babble, then speak) and security guard (as baby

safety basics for growing babies

SAFE AND SOUND

As babies jump, crawl, cruise and bounce from one developmental stage to another, the potential for trouble increases dramatically.

Continue to follow the baby safety basics, while keeping the following in mind, too:

■ Once babies are able to sit up without support, you may think they're sitting pretty – and safely. Think again. Early sitters can topple over without warning. Don't ever leave them alone in a sitting position or sit them on high surfaces without a supportive hand.

■ As babies learn to pick up small objects, anything within their reach may end up in their mouths. And that can lead to choking or poisoning. Always do a sweep of the area where baby is playing and remove any small objects lying around. This means no older children's Lego pieces or Barbie shoes, no coins or buttons, no hard sweets or cat biscuits – nothing toxic or small enough for baby to choke on.

■ Sure, baby's pulling-up trick is cute, but it can also be dangerous if you're not careful. You and the parents will have to do some adjusting. Watch out for unsturdy furniture and items on shelves that the baby can reach.

■ Once baby has mastered pulling up, cruising can't be far behind.

starts to poke her fingers in places they shouldn't go). The child in your care will amaze you with his daily feats and accomplishments as he grows from sleepy-lumpy infant to playful, active, into-everything baby. And by the time that baby is ready to celebrate her first birthday – probably toddling and yammering away – you'll be amazed at how far you and she have come since the first time you met.

To make sure she isn't cruising for a bruising, check all the furniture that she'll be pulling up on and holding on to and make sure it's stable. Don't let baby hang on to open dresser drawers, tables with sharp edges, swinging doors or chairs that can swivel, rock or topple over.

■ When baby reaches for something she shouldn't touch (whether it's a breakable dish or a hot stove), say firmly, 'No, don't touch that.' If it shouldn't be touched because it belongs to someone else, say so: 'Don't touch that. That's Daddy's book.' If it shouldn't be touched because it's dangerous, say so, too: 'Don't touch. That's hot. Ouch!' Then give baby something of his own to touch: 'This is Justin's toy' or 'This is Maddie's juice.'

■ Even if there's a gate at the top and bottom of stairs in the home, baby will still need (and want) to learn to scale the steps. Show him how to climb up and how to come down (tummy down, feet first). Continue to supervise climbing (and keep gates up), even when he becomes a pro.

■ Kids love to play in the water. Some love it so much that they'll try to jump in at the sight of a full bath, a pool or a pond. But babies can drown in even a couple of inches of water. Whenever you see water, hold baby firmly back and say, 'Wait for a grown-up.'

WHAT TO EXPECT

Babies change on almost a daily basis in the second six months. Here are some of the developments you can look forward to when caring for a baby six months to one year old:

- By the end of the seventh month, baby should be sitting without support. She can probably play peekaboo and may be starting to pick up small objects. Make sure all dangerous ones stay out of her reach!

- By the end of the eighth month, baby will be able to feed himself a cracker and may be able to get into a sitting position from his stomach. Some eight-month-olds are also crawling.

- Around nine months, baby will start to pull up to a standing position.

- By the end of the 10th month, baby will likely be cruising (walking while holding on to furniture). This means you'll need to keep her in 'safe' rooms where the furniture is sturdy enough to support her and close enough together to help her along.

- Around 11 months, babies start saying 'mama' and 'dada' – and maybe even your name (or some form of it). When this happens, you'll be as proud as the parents!

- Somewhere around their first birthday, some babies begin to take their first steps. Once walking begins, watch out: you've entered the Toddler Zone.

1 to 3 years

Lace up your sneakers and start your engines. From walking to running to climbing, a toddler is always on the move, keeping you on your toes (and feet!). And if caring for a toddler tests your stamina, it will also test your patience as you weather those famous temper tantrums, those endless nos, that trademark stubbornness and those crazy eating habits (yuck, the peas and potatoes are touching!). But here's the bright side, and a very bright side it is. You'll be warmed by huge toddler hugs and wet toddler kisses, tickled pink by that adorable toddler talk ('go-ba' for good-bye, 'sgetti' for spaghetti) and enchanted by all the cute things that toddlers do – sing along off-key to a favourite song, scribble with a crayon and call it a rainbow, feed you make-believe food from the pretend kitchen, dance whenever you play music, delight in water and sand play, try to throw a ball, put their clothes on backwards and their shoes on the wrong feet.

WHAT TO EXPECT

The toddler years are full of developmental milestones to look forward to.

THE ONE-YEAR-OLD. The days of putting the baby down in the middle of the floor and knowing she'll stay there are long gone. A one-year-old has graduated from babyhood (and sitting still) into toddlerhood (sit still? not me!). She'll be constantly amazing you with all of her latest accomplishments:

■ Sometime around (or soon after) her first birthday, she'll begin to walk on her own. And by the time the year is over, she'll probably be able to walk backwards and up steps.

safety basics for toddlers

SAFE AND SOUND

Not only will you have a harder time keeping up with the toddler (now that she can run away from you – fast), but you'll also have a harder time keeping her away from danger and preventing injuries (now that she can climb onto the kitchen counter and reach the upper cabinets). Review the safety tips on pages 22–25, adapting them to the age of the child you're caring for, and be sure to keep these additional safety basics in mind:

■ Never leave the toddler alone on a changing table, bed, couch or other furniture.

■ Always strap the toddler in a high chair, booster seat or pushchair.

■ Don't leave the toddler alone in a shopping trolley for even a minute. Make sure she's always strapped in.

■ Always strap the toddler into a forward-facing car seat in the back-seat of a car. Never, ever make an exception.

■ Don't let the toddler pet strange dogs, and don't leave a toddler alone with the family pet, even a friendly one. The most sweet-tempered dog can bite when a toddler tries to chase it or playfully pulls its tail.

■ Keep a watchful eye on a toddler with a balloon. If it pops, make sure there are no pieces left on the floor. A toddler can choke on them.

■ Never let a toddler play on or near stairs.

■ Don't let a toddler walk and eat at the same time. (See page 56 and 60 for more tips on safe eating.)

■ Never let a toddler walk alone across a road, even in a safe neighbourhood and even on a road that has few cars (such as a cul-de-sac).

■ Keep an eye on the toddler at all times while he's awake. Toddlers have the skills (climbing, opening cabinets, piling up books to reach something dangerous) and curiosity to get into all kinds of trouble.

■ Though a one-year-old is becoming more social, she'll still want to stay close to you most of the time.

■ A one-year-old will be able to recognize her own name. She will also recognize your name – and even use it!

■ As they near their second birthday, many one-year-olds will be able to speak a number of words (between 6 and 25, sometimes even more), and some children may even be linking words together to form 'sentences'. Still, few can express themselves clearly, which leads to frustration.

THE TWO-YEAR-OLD. Look who's talking – all the time! The two-year-old will be chatting the day away (though you may still not understand all of what he's saying). His favourite word is still sure to be 'no', his favourite phrase 'do it myself!' – but he also has many other new tricks up his sleeve:

■ Two-year-olds can move around (run, jump, hop, climb) with greater ease than before. They'll be faster, too – catch them if you can!

■ By the end of the year, some two-year-olds can dress themselves. Even if they're not very good at it, they may want to 'do it myself', which means the pants may sometimes go on backwards . . . and everything will take longer.

did you know?

Two-year-olds understand many more words than they can speak. They also understand more concepts than before (they know that both cats and dogs are animals, that rain makes you wet). What's more, they're also beginning to understand 'right' (petting the dog) from 'wrong' (pulling the dog's tail). But keep in mind that this doesn't mean they won't do 'wrong' things over and over again, since they have a hard time controlling impulses.

■ A two-year-old's attention span is increasing, so you'll be able to get through a whole book together or finish a puzzle – sometimes.

■ A two-year-old will use many words and speak in short sentences. He still won't be able to say everything that's on his mind and can still get frustrated when you don't understand him.

■ It may be potty time for some two-year-olds, though others won't be ready until age three.

■ Two-year-olds are becoming social animals who enjoy spending time with other children their age, though they may still do much of their play side by side.

THE THREE-YEAR-OLD. Who's curious? A three-year-old certainly is. She's busy exploring the world around her, a world that's getting bigger and more exciting as she takes on new adventures (playing with friends at nursery). She's more independent than ever (she can dress and feed herself, and probably use the potty) and is a joy to be around (most of the time).

■ A three-year-old is ready to take on the world (and probably even school!). She can kick a ball, climb stairs with ease, control crayons and shape play dough.

■ A three-year-old is super-smart – able to play matching games, thumb through a picture book, count fingers and toes.

■ A three-year-old loves being in the company of other children and starts making friends.

4 to 6 years

They're still as cute as buttons, but now they can do up the buttons all by themselves. They're still creative geniuses, but now their artwork is more likely to a) look like artwork, and b) decorate the paper instead of the walls. They may not be reading yet – but boy, can sure talk up a storm! And although they're still mastering the art of independence, they've probably stopped attaching themselves to your leg like human Velcro at the school door.

Yet as far as infant-school children have come since their baby and toddler days, don't be fooled into thinking they're all grown up. They've got a lot of maturing to do, and a lot of learning. But with temper tantrums and negativity (mostly) behind them, and with their social skills sharpening, you'll find that they are delightful (mostly) to be around – interesting and interested, fascinating and fascinated, loving and lovable.

WHAT TO EXPECT

THE FOUR-YEAR-OLD. Now that they can ride a trike, jump and play catch, four-year-olds are on the move all day, but at a more organized, less frantic pace than toddlers. And because they're better at expressing themselves with words and at controlling their emotions, they're less likely to become frustrated. Four-year-olds will be able to do the following – or will try their darnedest:

■ Write their own name

■ Draw a face

■ Cut paper with blunt scissors

■ Unbutton buttons; use buckles or laces

■ Use the toilet alone

■ Catch a bouncing ball

■ Pump their legs to keep a swing going

■ Take turns (and do it even without being reminded)

teaching right from left

TRICKS OF THE TRADE

Need an easy way to teach an infant-school child his right from his left? Show him that when he holds up the thumb and index finger of his left hand, they form the letter L – for 'left'. Not only will he be able to remember which side is which, but he'll also get to know his letters better (or at least one of them!).

- Tell the difference between something real and pretend

- Act out a made-up 'play'

- Use proper grammar often

- Enjoy rhyming and nonsense words

- Separate from their parents without crying (most of the time)

- Like to play with other children

- Play tag, hide-and-seek and other games with simple rules

- Hop on one foot

THE FIVE-YEAR-OLD. Gone is that adorable potbelly, the last leftover of toddlerhood. In its place comes a slimmer, more mature-looking, more independent child. Five-year-olds can be expected to do the following:

- Argue when they don't get their own way

- Be harder to distract

- Love to draw, make art projects and show off their work

- Write their own name

- Know their right from their left

- Show interest in reading and letters

- Get dressed and undressed by themselves (though you may still need to help with zips, laces and small buttons)

- Eat neatly (sort of) with fork and spoon

- Play nicely with peers and make friendships (often picking a 'best friend')

- Plan activities

- Be bossy

- Engage in a lot of dramatic and imaginative play

- Be eager to please parents and carers

- Skip and jump rope

- Ride a bicycle (with or without training wheels)

- Attempt activities that require complex coordination (swimming, football, roller skating)

- Remember stories and repeat them back

- Draw pictures of people and animals

- Concentrate well

- Understand the concept of time

- Be sensitive to others' feelings

THE SIX-YEAR-OLD. Lucky for you, a six-year-old is settling down and isn't as active as a Reception-age child. Unlucky for you, a six-year-old may also become moodier, going from giddy to angry in a matter of minutes. Six-year-olds will typically do the following:

- Create art masterpieces (using scissors, coloured paper, markers, glue, and so on)

- Be very curious

- Interact well with people

- Think logically

- Understand the concept of cause and effect

- Change best friends and enemies frequently

- Be bossy

- Be competitive with peers

- Find ways to be the centre of attention

- Be sensitive and cry easily

- Be attached to a teacher

safety basics for young children

SAFE AND SOUND

As this age group achieves more independence and starts spending less time by your side (and clinging to your legs), you'll need to redouble your efforts to keep them safe. Review the safety tips on pages 22–25 and 28, adapting them to the age of the child you're caring for, and be sure to keep these additional safety basics in mind:

■ Remind the child never to invite anyone into the house without the permission of a parent or carer.

■ Remind the child of her telephone number and home address, and how to dial 999.

■ Remind the child never to give out personal information over the phone to strangers (except when talking to 999).

■ Never leave a young child alone in the house, in the car or at a store, park or other public place – even for a moment.

■ Always accompany the child to the toilet in a public place.

■ Always strap young children into a booster seat in the backseat of a car. Never make an exception.

the special-needs child

Caring for any child is a big responsibility. But if the child has a developmental disability (autism, cerebral palsy, epilepsy or mental retardation, for example), your responsibility is even greater. Understanding and learning about the disability will make your job easier.

The parents will be able to answer most of the questions you'll have about what makes their child's care different, including basic information on the disability, best ways to communicate with the child, special equipment the child might need (and that you'll need to learn how to use), behaviour or symptoms to watch out for, any special feeding instructions or other specific recommendations. Before you go it solo, you'll want to spend plenty of time with parent and child, watching their interaction and learning hands-on how various situations are managed.

Remember that special-needs children also have the same needs that other children have — to be nurtured, cared for and loved just the way they are.

◆ ◆ ◆

feeding

filling small tummies (at least with the right kinds of foods) can be a big challenge. And it's not just about the food. Sure, a nutritious diet helps to power a child's busy day and all that growing that's going on. But also on the menu is learning – that bringing cup to mouth without spilling half the juice takes a steady hand, that the oat circles don't stay on the spoon when you turn it over, that the shape those sandwiches are cut into is called a square. What's more, mealtime is a time for fun (applesauce makes a great dip for chicken fingers . . . and baby fingers!) and for socializing (who cares if all the milk drips down my face when I smile back at you?). *Bon appétit!*

newborn to 6 months

WHAT'S BABY EATING?

Some mums choose to pump breast milk to fill the daily bottles. Other parents choose to use formula. And some combine the two. This is what you need to know about what you'll be feeding baby:

EXPRESSED BREAST MILK. Expressing breast milk at work (or even at home to store for later) takes a mum a lot of time and effort. Your job is to make sure the precious milk gets to its target properly and safely. Here's how:

■ **Defrost it.** If the milk you're using is frozen, shake the bottle or bag under lukewarm tap water until it's defrosted and then use it within 30 minutes. Or let the milk defrost overnight in the fridge and use within 24 hours.

■ **Chill it.** Keep expressed milk refrigerated until you plan to feed it to the baby. Freshly expressed breast milk can be kept for up to 48 hours in the fridge.

■ **Pour it.** Pour only what you will need into the bottle. Refrigerate the rest for a later feeding.

■ **Warm it.** If the baby likes her bottle warm, place it in a bowl of hot water or run hot water over it. Never microwave the bottle, because the liquid may warm unevenly and possibly burn the baby's mouth.

■ **Test it.** Check the temperature of the milk by shaking a few drops on your inner wrist; it's ready for use when it no longer feels cold to the touch. It doesn't need to be very warm, just body temperature.

■ **Toss it.** If there is leftover milk at the end of a bottle feeding, throw it away; it's not safe to use later.

BREAST-FEEDING SUPPORT

Q *'The baby I lookafter drinks only breast milk; his mother pumps at work during the day. Is there any way I can make it easier for her?'*

A Pumping on the job is hard work – and mums need all the help they can get. Fortunately, there are several ways you can lend a hand. First, when Mum returns from work, offer to transfer the breast milk to the fridge or freezer, and put the ice packs she's used to keep the milk cold back in the freezer. If the pump needs washing, you can offer to do that, too. In the morning you can volunteer to pack the pump or put the frozen ice packs back in the insulated bag.

Another way to help is to avoid calling her (unless you have to) when the baby is crying. Often a nursing mother will begin to leak breast milk when she hears her baby cry – not exactly convenient if she's working.

did you know?

Thought milk was always white? Breast milk is actually bluish or yellowish in color. What's more, when frozen or refrigerated, breast milk will separate into milk and cream. Just shake gently to mix before feeding.

breast milk checklist

DO	DON'T
☑ **DO START WITH THE OLDER MILK.** Use the frozen breast milk with the oldest dates first. (Breast milk stays fresh in a standard freezer for about three months.)	☒ **DON'T DEFROST THE WRONG WAY.** Don't thaw out the frozen breast milk in a microwave, on top of the stove or at room temperature.
☑ **DO KEEP SAFETY IN MIND.** Throw away any milk that has been stored for longer than the recommended amount of time.	☒ **DON'T REFREEZE THAWED BREAST MILK.** Refrigerate it, and if baby doesn't drink it within 24 hours, toss it.

have bottle, will travel

Keep these tips in mind when feeding a baby on the go:

■ If the baby is formula-fed, take along ready-to-use bottled formula or bottles of water and single-serving formula packets to mix with them. (Remember to ask the parents first, since ready-to-use formula is very expensive.)

■ Store prepared bottles in an insulated container or in a plastic bag with a small ice pack.

■ If the prepared formula or breast milk isn't cold to the touch when you take it out of the insulated bag, don't use it. (It's fine to use unopened single servings that aren't cold.)

FORMULA. Is formula on the baby's menu? Remember the following when preparing, storing and feeding.

■ **Mix it.** Follow the directions on the label precisely when mixing formula with water, and use the enclosed measuring scoop for powdered formula.

■ **Warm it.** When warming the bottle, place it in a bowl of hot water or run hot water over it. (Never heat formula in a microwave oven, because the liquid may warm up unevenly or become hot enough to burn a baby's mouth.) Keep in mind that not all parents will want you to warm the bottle. Babies can drink formula right out of the fridge or at room temperature.

■ **Check it.** Test the temperature of the formula by shaking a few drops on your inner wrist. It's ready for use when it no longer feels cold to the touch. It doesn't need to be very warm, just body temperature.

■ **Serve it.** Once warm, the formula must be used right away. Germs can grow fast in warm formula.

■ **Store it.** Keep prepared (unused) bottles refrigerated until ready to use, but not for longer than 48 hours.

■ **Toss it.** If the baby doesn't finish the whole bottle, throw away leftover formula. It's not safe to reuse, even if you refrigerate it.

formula checklist

DO

☑ **DO CHECK THE LABEL.** Always check the expiration date on a can or carton of formula.

☑ **DO START CLEAN.** Wash your hands and the top of formula cans with detergent and hot water before opening; rinse well and dry.

☑ **DO FINISH CLEAN.** Rinse bottles and teats right after use for easier cleaning.

DON'T

☒ **DON'T KEEP FORMULA TOO LONG.** Never use any formula that has expired.

☒ **DON'T ADD WATER TO FORMULA IF THE LABEL DOESN'T SAY TO.** Adding water when it's not needed or not adding the right amount of water can make the baby sick.

☒ **DON'T FREEZE FORMULA.**

did you know?

Feedings don't just fill the belly – they fill a baby's need for love and attention. So don't forget to cuddle, smile and coo when you're feeding. And keep that eye contact going!

BOTTLE FEEDING – THE BASICS

It seems easy enough: fill up a bottle, give the bottle to the baby, she drinks it all up. Presto – you're done. But feeding a baby isn't always that easy. There will be times when the baby's crying too hard to start sucking, or when she spits up three or four times during a feeding (all over you, of course). Here are some ways to make feeding time an easier time every time:

WASH UP. Before baby's meal, wash your hands well with soap and water.

GET COMFY. Sit in a chair that supports your back and place a pillow under the arm that's holding baby.

QUIET, PLEASE. Make mealtime a peaceful time. That means no TV, loud music or other noise that could distract baby from the bottle. If there are older siblings around, set them up with a quiet activity (such as colouring or a puzzle) before you begin. Or have them sit beside you so you can read them a quiet story.

MAKE A CHANGE. If baby is calm and not crying with hunger, you've got time for a nappy change. Not only will a clean nappy make for a more comfortable meal, but it will also allow you to put baby down for a nap right away if he falls asleep at the end of the feeding.

COOL BABY DOWN. We're talking temper here, not temperature. A baby who is extremely fussy or crying very hard will have trouble settling down for a meal (and will probably swallow a lot of air, which will lead to wind pain and more crying). To calm her down, try rocking or singing a soothing song first.

RING THE DINNER BELL. Let baby know it's chow time with this little trick: Stroke his cheek with your finger or the tip of the bottle's teat. Once his mouth is open, gently place the teat between his lips and watch for happy sucking. If he still doesn't get the picture, placing a drop of formula or breast milk on his lips should clue him in.

DON'T PROP. A propped bottle means baby misses out on the social time (with you) that is a vital part of feeding. It's also dangerous, since a baby can choke when the bottle's propped, even if she's in a reclining high chair or infant seat. So be sure to hold baby in your arms while feeding her.

AVOID AIR. Too much air during a feeding is a recipe for gassiness with a side of crying. To keep air out of baby's tummy, tilt the bottle up so that the liquid completely fills the teat.

BREAK FOR A BURP. A switch of sides mid-feeding gives baby a chance to see the world (and your face, one of baby's favourite views) from a different angle. It will also keep your arms from cramping

did you know?

Young babies usually get their full quota of fluids from breast milk or formula – they don't need extra water. In fact, drinking water fills babies up, making them too stuffed to get the nutrients they need from their feedings. So don't give an infant any water between meals unless the parents have asked you to.

up. An added bonus: it will remind you to stop to wind baby (see page 181 for winding positions).

LET BABY CALL IT QUITS. When it comes to feedings, baby's the boss. If she seems finished after taking only four ounces (and the usual meal is six), see if a burp is in order (it may be gas, not food, that's filling that little tummy). If she still doesn't want more, don't be tempted to push the rest of the bottle. A healthy baby knows when to stop. As long as she's happy, gaining enough weight, and wetting and dirtying enough nappies, you can be sure she's getting enough to eat.

Q *'The parents have told me that I should feed their baby boy on demand. But I've raised three children of my own and have always fed them on a schedule. Would it be all right to question the parents on this?'*

A Your mission (if you've agreed to accept it) is to support the parents in their child-rearing decisions, whether or not you agree with them. That doesn't mean you shouldn't talk things over (preferably when you both have enough time to really talk), if only to get a better idea of why the parents feel the way they do. In the case of demand feeding, chances are that they've read – or have heard from the paediatrician – that feeding a

---

TRICKS OF THE TRADE

check your speed limit

How fast – or slow – should formula or breast milk flow from a bottle? You can check the speed of a teat by turning the bottle upside down. If milk pours or spurts out, it's flowing too quickly. If just a drop or two escapes, it's too slow. Baby's best bet: a little spray and then some drops.

If the hole seems to be the wrong size, tell the parents so they can provide you with new teats.

baby when he's hungry helps him thrive. This is particularly true if he's on breast milk; since it's digested faster, babies on breast milk need to be fed more often. Demand feeding also lets a baby know that his needs matter in the world, which makes him feel more secure.

Of course, crying doesn't always indicate that baby's demanding a feeding. As you already know, babies cry for many other reasons (see page 136).

TIME FOR SOLIDS

Q *'Whenever I'm eating, the five-month-old I care for tries to grab my fork out of my hand. Her parents haven't started her on solids yet, but I think she's trying to tell me it's time. What should I do? Tell the parents?'*

A Spread the news! Parents would love to hear about this interest in eating – one of the signs that a baby's ready to start solids. Assuming that the baby has shown other signs of readiness (for instance, can she hold her head up well when propped to sit?) and that the doctor has given the go-ahead, it may be time to grab a bib and get started on those solids. On the other hand, the parents may be following a doctor's recommendation to wait until their daughter is six months old to make the momentous move to spoon feeding. If that's the case, just keep the baby happy with her bottle for now. And get ready for the mess you'll be dealing with soon enough!

6 to 12 months

That big moment has arrived: baby's graduation from a liquid diet. Around six months (sometimes a little earlier, sometimes a little later), babies will start on solid foods: first mushed, followed by mashed, then smashed. Before you know it, you and the baby will be choosing from the same lunchtime menu.

did you know?

Can't imagine life without sugar, salt and fast food? Babies who have never had them don't know what they're missing, and that's a good thing. They're all extras babies can – and should – do without. So don't offer the baby fries from your plate or a bite of your doughnut or, for that matter, even tiny tastes of any foods that the parents haven't okayed.

FEEDING SOLIDS – THE BASICS

Beginners don't eat much – and they don't need to. They're still getting most of their nutritional needs filled through the breast or bottle. The quality of the eating experience is much more important than the quantity of food they eat. Here's how to make mealtime fun, while keeping it safe:

FEED, DON'T FORCE. As soon as the baby tells you he's had enough to eat – by spitting out the food or turning his head – call it quits for that meal. Jamming the spoon into his mouth when he's not hungry will make the high chair a battleground, which can lead to more complicated eating problems later on.

HAVE A CONVERSATION. Talk to the baby as you feed her. Agree with her that the carrots are delicious. Ask if you can have a bite of her stewed pear (but only pretend to; never eat from baby's spoon). Or tell her how lovely she looks covered in strained apricots.

DON'T DOUBLE-DIP. Take what you'll need out of the jar and put it in a dish. If you serve directly from the jar, the spoon that's been in the baby's mouth and dipped back in the jar will carry germs with it. If you ever do use the jar as your serving dish, you'll have to throw away whatever you don't use at that feeding.

CHECK THE TEMPERATURE. Some babies take their food at room temperature; others like it a tad warmer. If you've been told to warm the baby's food, place the container or bowl in hot water (don't use a microwave, which can heat food unevenly). Test the temperature – use a spoon to dab a drop on your fingertip, but don't stick your finger in the food – before serving it up. (Don't forget to heat up only a small portion so there are no leftovers to toss.)

KEEP IT SOFT. Stick to foods that soften or dissolve or foods that can be gummed. Cut food into pea-size cubes or chunks. Serve (as they're introduced) soft, ripe fruits; vegetables cooked until they're soft; soft, crumbled meat; well-cooked pasta; cheeses.

THINK SMALL. Whatever you're serving, put out only a little at a time. If you give baby too much food at once, it may all go in his mouth in one fistful – or, more likely, it may all end up on the floor.

HOLD THE MEAT?

Q *'The parents I work for are vegetarians, but I'm not. Is it okay for me to bring a meat sandwich once in a while for my own lunch?'*

A Many vegetarians think of their meat-free diet as their personal choice, and nothing more. Some, however, don't like the idea of having meat in their home (even when it's neatly tucked into a sandwich). So just ask. If it turns out they'd like to keep their home meat-free, save the ham-and-cheese for dinner.

SAFE AND SOUND

testing, testing

Many parents will want to introduce new foods slowly into their baby's diet, just one at a time with a few days in between. Follow their plan carefully. This way, if there is an allergic reaction, you'll all be able to figure out which food brought it on.

SAFE AND SOUND

no honey, honey

Never serve honey (or foods that contain honey) to a baby under a year old. It could make her very sick.

FOOD ALLERGIES

Q '*The baby I take care of is allergic to wheat. Obviously I would never give him anything that I know has wheat in it, but I'm afraid that someday I'll make a mistake and give him the wrong food. The situation is making me very nervous.*'

A Dealing with a child's food allergies can make even his parents anxious. After all, ingredients like wheat can show up in the strangest places (would you believe, sauces!). Don't worry, though – once you get the hang of it, watching out for wheat (or other allergenic foods) will become second nature.

First, you'll need to get the lowdown on the allergy from the parents. Second, you'll need to become an expert label reader (again, ask the parents what to look out for). Third, you'll have to do a lot of explaining (when you're out to play, you'll have to make sure other parents and carers know not to hand the baby a cracker; when you're eating out with baby, you'll have to get the lowdown about what's in the food before it's served).

Finally, if it's a severe allergy, you'll need to know what to do in case the baby has a reaction. Having a plan in place will put your mind at ease.

OFF THE MENU

Until babies become experts at chewing and swallowing, certain foods can cause them to choke. So remember to keep the foods listed below (plus the ones on page 56) away from the baby in your care:

- Raisins and other dried fruits (unless they're cooked and cut up)

- Crisps
- Whole peas and beans (unless they're very soft)
- Raw firm vegetables (carrots, celery or peppers, for instance)
- Chunks of meat or chicken
- Large chunks of cheese

WHAT GOES IN MUST COME OUT

Starting to make some interesting discoveries in baby's nappy? Not to worry. The colour, smell and texture of a baby's bowel movements will change when he starts eating solid foods.

easy mealtimes

Hitting the mark – in other words, getting food into baby's mouth – is the hard part. Make the rest of the meal as easy on yourself as possible with these tips:

TRICKS OF THE TRADE

- **PLAN FOR EASIER CLEANUPS.** Room temperature permitting, feed the baby in a nappy only. Use an extra-large bib (or, for really easy cleanup, use a disposable one). Lay yesterday's newspaper or a plastic mat on the floor to catch spills. Wipe up right after the meal, before the smeared peas and cottage cheese get hard and crusty.

- **GIVE BABY A SPOON.** A baby won't be as likely to try to grab the one you're steering toward her mouth if she has one of her own to wave around.

- **KEEP IT COOL.** Unless the parents have told you otherwise, don't get the baby used to eating foods that have been warmed up. Feeding solids at room temperature or even straight from the refrigerator is perfectly fine for baby and much easier for you.

- **KEEP IT SAFE.** Eating and running (or crawling) is dangerous. Serve up all food (even snacks) in the high chair or, later, a booster seat.

Many foods will be hard for him to digest – and may come out looking pretty much like they did going in (especially foods like blueberries and corn). Others break down in unexpected ways (for instance, oat cereals can turn stool sandy). One red flag to check for in baby's nappy once solids have been started: stools that have lots of mucus in them or are unusually runny. This might mean a new food is not agreeing with his system. If that happens, alert the parents.

FOODS FOR TINY FINGERS

Once a baby masters the grip that brings food and mouth together (sometime around the eighth or ninth month), a whole new world of eating (and independence) will open up: finger foods. Check with the parents about which to give and when. Here are some favourites for young self-feeders:

■ Easily dissolving crackers that baby can gum, like rice cakes

■ Teething biscuits

■ Cheerios or other oat circles

■ Well-cooked fruit wedges

■ Ripe avocado slices

INTRODUCING... THE CUP

Parents will probably introduce the cup to their baby sometime during the second half of the first year – and they'll

don't have a cow

SAFE AND SOUND

A baby will continue drinking formula or breast milk until his first birthday. After that, he'll probably be started on full fat cow's milk. Cow's milk, which is hard to digest, should never be given to a baby before the age of 12 months. It can lead to diarrhoea and allergies.

don't be loose with the juice

SAFE AND SOUND

Once juice is started, the baby will probably be limited to four to six ounces a day. More than that, and she won't have room for her bottles of breast milk or formula, or for solids. Another problem with too much juice (even for older kids): It can cause diarrhoea, stomachaches and bloating – no fun for anyone. One way to make that juice last longer: mix juice half-and-half with water.

probably want you to help coach him through some cup practice during the day. When you do, keep these pointers in mind:

START WITH THE RIGHT STUFF. For practice sessions, it makes sense to begin with small sips of water (which will be less messy when it rolls down baby's chin, which it will). After baby has mastered water, you can progress (with the parents' okay) to the messier stuff: small amounts of formula or breast milk, or juice mixed with water.

KEEP IT FUN. Get baby excited about the cup itself. If it's covered with cartoon characters, point out the friends on the cup who are waiting for her to take a sip. If the cup is clear, swirl the liquid around and get a good giggle going.

PREPARE FOR A WET TIME. Unless you're using a non-spill sippy cup (and parents may want you to limit use of these cups, or to alternate with a regular cup), expect that baby (and possibly you) will get wet. Though it may be tempting to keep baby dry by holding the cup yourself, it's more important for him to practise doing the holding – even if practice hasn't made perfect yet.

EXPECT LESS. Baby will probably get very little of the contents of the cup into her mouth at first. Once she hits her cup stride, however, more will go where it's supposed to.

DRINK WITH BABY. Babies learn by watching the adults around them. And they love to do what you do – or what their big brother or sister does. If you teach by example ('Look at my cup!'), baby will catch on.

APPLAUSE, PLEASE. Baby will love to know how proud you are. So cheer those sips on!

1 to 3 years

Think getting a spoonful of cereal into a baby's mouth is tricky? You ain't seen nothin' yet. Toddlers have strange eating habits (make that bizarre). Getting a meal into them can be time-consuming and frustrating. But not to worry. As long as the toddler is growing, healthy and happy, she's getting enough to eat. So don't push, don't nag – and definitely don't pick food fights.

FEEDING TODDLERS – THE BASICS

No one ever said getting a toddler to eat is easy (at least no one who's ever tried it).

Most toddlers are picky, unpredictable eaters who'd much rather run around and test the patience of the authority figure (you) than eat. A challenge? Yes. Impossible? No. Follow these suggestions, and you'll be on the road to dining success:

TRY, TRY AGAIN. Offer new foods next to old favourites. And don't give up after one try. A food that's flat-out rejected twice may be happily gobbled up the fifth time it's offered.

WATCH WHAT YOU EAT. You know it's important to be on your best behaviour when caring for a toddler (you certainly don't want him to copy any bad habits), but did you know the same holds true for eating? If the toddler sees you chomping on chips and candy, he'll want some, too. Eat healthy foods (at least in front of the child) and encourage your toddler to be a copy kitten.

DON'T COOK ALONE. Toddlers love to 'help' cook. If they're involved in the prep process (from picking the food out at the store to stirring it up in the kitchen), they'll be more likely to dig in at mealtime. Of course, don't let small children cut with sharp knives or get close to hot stoves or other kitchen dangers.

FEED BY THE CLOCK. Even if they were fed on demand as babies, toddlers need to eat meals at regular times. Otherwise, they'll graze the day away and never have room for a full meal. Schedule a snack between each mealtime – tiny tummies can't go too long without a fill-up.

QUIET DOWN. A peaceful activity (like reading a story) will help a toddler settle down before a meal.

NO DISTRACTIONS. Focus on the meal when it's time to eat. That means no TV in the background and no toys on the table. A healthy serving of conversation, however, makes every meal a whole lot more fun – so chat up the toddler while he eats.

GET COMFORTABLE. A child who's uncomfortable isn't likely to eat well. Make sure the high chair or booster seat is comfy. Serve food on child-sized plates, and give the toddler forks and spoons with handles that are easy for little fingers to use.

MAKE EATING FUN. Healthful eating doesn't have to be boring. Cut those sandwiches into interesting shapes. Put alphabet noodles in the vegetable soup. Serve up some French toast fingers. Or arrange food in the shape of a funny face or an animal. (For fun recipes, see pages 63–65.)

GIVE THE TODDLER CONTROL. Allow the toddler to decide how much to eat (or not eat). Never push food or turn a meal into a battle. And never make a fuss if the child refuses to eat anything at all. A healthy toddler who's never pushed will eat as much as he needs.

BUT NOT TOO MUCH CONTROL. If the toddler refuses to eat at lunchtime, don't give him any other food until the next scheduled snacktime (though it's fine to make that snack more filling than usual).

LET THE MESS FALL WHERE IT MAY. When you're two years old, eating isn't just about filling your tummy. It's also about experiencing your food – squishing it between your fingers, squashing it with your spoon and, every now and then, hurling it through the air. Be prepared for some of the food to end up in the child's hair, on her lap, on the walls. With any luck, most of it will land in her mouth.

SEND THE RIGHT MESSAGE. Toddlers should eat only when they're hungry. Try not to confuse food with love, discipline or comfort. Don't offer a cracker to calm down an upset toddler. Don't celebrate with a biscuit to reward a good deed. Don't bribe a cranky toddler with a piece of chocolate. And never even think about withholding food from a hungry toddler as a form of punishment.

FICKLE EATERS

Q *'The toddler I care for will ask for something to eat and then, after I prepare it for him, change his mind and ask for something else. I'm tired of being a short-order cook!'*

A It's perfectly okay to let a toddler choose what he wants to eat – within limits.

Limit #1: Offer only healthy options (keep in mind that cereal with milk is just as healthy an option for dinner as meat and potatoes, especially when it's served up with some fruit).

Limit #2: Offer only two options (too many choices are overwhelming for small children).

Limit #3: Once a choice has been made, the toddler has to stick with it. (Learning how to make choices is an important life skill, but so is learning to live with them.) If the child has asked for pancakes but turns them down once they're on the table, don't head back to the kitchen to scramble eggs. Let him

---

snack attack

TRICKS OF THE TRADE

Toddlers need snacks to get them through the day. But since they have tiny tummies, it's never a good idea to fill them up with snacks that aren't nutritious. Here are some healthy snack ideas:

■ Bananas, especially yummy frozen (but peel before freezing)

■ Small boxes or zip-lock bags of whole-grain cereals (such as Cheerios)

■ Homemade mini muffins

■ Mini bagels

■ Cheese cubes or sticks

■ Whole-wheat, low-salt crackers

■ Rice cakes

■ Whole-grain biscuits or cereal bars

■ Sliced apple, spread very thinly with smooth peanut butter (if allowed)

know (kindly, calmly, but firmly) that he can have the pancakes he asked for (maybe with a little yogurt dip to make them more fun) – or wait for the next meal or snack.

Of course, a toddler may be less likely to turn down a meal if he's helped to prepare it, maybe by stirring the batter for pancakes and then watching them (from a safe distance!) cook up in the skillet. Adding a blueberry smiley face may seal the deal – who can say no to a pancake that's smiling back at you?

no-worry eating for toddlers

Just because a toddler can feed himself doesn't mean you can leave him alone at mealtimes. For social reasons as well as safety ones, always stay nearby. And always keep these other safety tips in mind.

■ Until a child is at least four, don't offer foods that pose a choking risk:

SAFE AND SOUND

- ☐ nuts or seeds (such as pumpkin or sunflower)
- ☐ large chunks of raw apples or carrots
- ☐ raisins and other dried fruits (unless cut up)
- ☐ whole grapes
- ☐ popcorn, hard sweets, gum
- ☐ hot dogs (unless skinned and cut into small pieces)
- ☐ peanut butter (unless there is no allergy and the peanut butter is very thinly spread)

■ Be sure meat, poultry and fish are served well-cooked. No rare burgers, no pink chicken, no sushi.

■ Don't serve a toddler raw or undercooked eggs or anything made with raw eggs (no batter licking!).

■ Stick to pasteurized milk and juice (never 'raw').

■ Keep the kitchen clean and germ-free by wiping counters, stoves and sinks with soapy water or cleansers (kept well out of reach of a curious toddler).

WHAT'S THE TODDLER EATING?

Toddlers are growing, but not as quickly as they did when they were babies. And since slower growth means less food is needed, don't be surprised when the toddler's appetite takes a dive. That's normal. Another reason for a slowdown in eating: toddlers don't like to sit still for a meal. They have bigger fish to fry than the kind you eat!

WHAT'S THE TODDLER DRINKING?

MILK. A one-year-old will probably be drinking full fat cow's milk (unless there's an allergy) until the age of two, when he may be switched to semi-skimmed milk, depending on what the parents prefer and on what the doctor has ordered.

JUICE. Even 100% fruit juices should be limited to no more than six ounces a day (that's less than a cup, total). They can't compare with whole fruit when it comes to nutrients and fibre content, and in excess they can cause diarrhoea, gas, bloating and stomach pain. Don't use a bottle of juice as a pacifier, and don't let a toddler drink from a sippy cup filled with juice all day. Diluting juice half-and-half with water makes it last longer and is easier on those teeth! Diluting with sparkling water makes juice more fun and festive.

BYE-BYE BOTTLE

Some parents wean their children from the bottle right after their first birthday. Others wait a few months; still others wait much longer. When the time comes for a toddler to kick the bottle, here are some ways to help things along:

REPLACE IT. Start out by dropping one bottle feeding and replacing it with a cup feeding. After a few days of adjustment, replace another bottle feeding with a cup feeding.

CUT BACK. Put less milk in the bottle than usual, and pour the rest into a cup. Each day, decrease the amount of milk in the bottle and increase the amount in the cup.

WATER ONLY. Serve only water in the bottle, starting with one feeding at a time. Save milk, formula or juice for the cup. The child might find that the bottles aren't worth it anymore. But make sure she gets enough milk or formula from the cup.

SIT 'EM DOWN. Some parents allow toddlers to drink from the bottle only when they're sitting down. Since toddlers hate sitting still, that's often reason enough for them to give up the bottle.

HIDE THE BOTTLE. When you give a child a cup, put the bottle away. This way, he won't be crying for the bottle on the counter while you're pushing the cup.

PRACTISE PATIENCE. The transition from bottle to cup may take a few weeks, even a month or two. At first it will be hard for everyone, but don't give in and hand back the bottle when the going gets rough. Set a slow pace

muscle foods

TRICKS OF THE TRADE

Have a picky eater on your hands? Try using a little 'muscle'. Toddlers and preschoolers are much more likely to open wide for foods that they know will make them 'big and strong' (two things every young child wants to be!). So instead of pushing or pleading (which never work anyway), talk about how milk, cheese and yogurt will give him healthy bones, how chicken and beans will build muscles, how carrots will help him see better (especially at night), how broccoli will help him jump higher and run faster – and how all these 'body buddies' will help him grow!

and stick with the programme. Eventually, the child will get the message that the bottle is yesterday's news.

CUDDLE MORE. Many toddlers use the bottle as their comfort object – it calms them down and makes them feel safe. So be sure to give extra hugs, spend lots of laptime together and provide an extra serving of love when you take the bottle away. It will make the transition easier.

4 to 6 years

Mealtimes shared with a young child should be fun for both of you. A happy atmosphere at the table means not only fewer food fights now, but better eating habits as the child grows older.

FEEDING – THE BASICS

Here are some tips to make all meals happy meals:

PREP TOGETHER. Increasing the child's participation in meal preparation will increase his interest in new or unfamiliar foods. Have him shell peas. Show him how to wash lettuce or scrub carrots.

EAT (HEALTHY) TOGETHER. A child who sees you lunching healthfully next to her (enjoying every bite!) will want to model your good eating habits.

TALK ABOUT FOOD. Teach the child about where foods come from and how they're grown. Also point out how healthful foods help him get big and strong. The more interesting you make a food sound, the more appealing it will be. Plus, you'll turn meals into a learning experience.

OFFER VARIETY. Serve up a variety of colours and textures to create interest and increase the number of foods the child will try and accept.

MAKE A LITTLE DIPPER. Serve vegetables and fruit with a healthy dip for flavour, nutrition and fun. Dip steamed broccoli in cheese sauce, pineapple slices in yogurt, chicken fingers in tomato sauce.

GO FOR SMALL. Big portions are overwhelming to small tummies. Keep portions child-sized.

SERVE ON TIME. Don't wait until the child is overtired, hungry or cranky to serve a meal. Keep to a dependable schedule for meals and snacks so the child knows when to expect them.

GIVE CHOICES. Allow the child to choose between two healthy meal suggestions (so she has a feeling of control) and let her decide whether or not to eat everything on her plate.

MAKE IT FUN. Serve food that's fun to eat. See the end of this chapter for some recipe ideas.

KEEP IT CALM. This means no TV or radio blaring in the background. It also means don't cry over the child's spilled milk or complain if there are leftovers at the end of the meal.

no-worry eating for young children

Even though this age group has a full set of chewing choppers, you'll still need to play it safe with foods:

SAFE AND SOUND

■ Slice hot dogs into quarters (lengthwise).

■ Remove bones from fish.

■ Remove pits from cherries, plums and peaches.

■ Continue to spread peanut butter thinly; never allow a child to eat peanut butter straight from the jar.

■ Continue to serve meat and poultry well-cooked.

■ Serve food up only when the child is sitting down.

WHAT'S ON THE MENU?

Like the toddler, the infant-school child needs to eat a well-balanced, varied diet. Like the toddler, too, he's likely to eat in stops and spurts (like a truck driver one day, like a sparrow the next).

Although this age group may be more willing than toddlers to try new foods, it won't always be easy to convince them to eat what's put in front of them. But this doesn't mean you should give up trying. The early school years are an ideal time to start teaching a child about lifelong healthy eating habits. Arm yourself with these suggestions:

■ Serve vitamin-rich foods as often as possible, including those high in vitamin C (berries, kiwi, pineapple, oranges, red pepper) and vitamin A (dried apricots, peaches, carrots, broccoli, lettuce, sweet potato, mango). Remember that fruit adds as much nutrition as green vegetables.

■ Got milk? Some young children lap up the white stuff; others snub it. If the child in your care doesn't like milk, no need to push. Cheese and yogurt are good substitutes.

■ Think cheese, fish, meat or chicken when looking for a protein push. Lucky for you, kids usually gobble them up.

■ Avoid high-sugar, high-fat foods (sweet desserts, sweets, sugared drinks, colas, chips, sausages, and so on). They don't call it junk food for nothing.

■ Start a One-Bite Club, where members are encouraged to taste all food served. No need to take another bite unless the first goes down happily.

■ Snacks matter. Serve snacks that are high in nutrients and low in added sugar. Small pieces of fruits and vegetables (served with dip for fun), whole-grain cereals, cheese cubes, tiny sandwiches and milk or juice are all good choices. A yogurt smoothie (fruit, yogurt and some juice, pureed in the blender) makes a nutritious treat.

don't go pop over fizz

Sugar-loaded soft drinks are filling and provide only empty calories. And each time a child reaches for a bottle of these bubblies, he's missing the opportunity to eat or drink something healthy. Besides, kids who drink fizzy drinks are much more likely to become fat and get cavities now – and later in life.

If the parents agree, follow these suggestions for cutting back on sugary soft drinks:

SAFE AND SOUND

■ KEEP FIZZY DRINKS OUT OF THE HOUSE. Don't buy them when running errands at the supermarket.

■ DON'T REACH FOR FIZZY DRINKS WHEN YOU'RE OUT. If the child is thirsty after a long day at school or a day in the park, stop for a bottle of water or a carton of milk.

■ NEVER USE FIZZY DRINKS AS A REWARD OR BRIBE. An extra five minutes on the swings is more fun, anyway.

■ BE A FIZZY DRINKS-SKIPPER. Don't let the child catch you slurping down that can of Coke. Let him see you drinking a glass of water or milk instead (it's good for you, too!).

■ MAKE JUICE SPRITZERS. Bubbly but nutritious, juice mixed half-and-half with sparkling water is a yummy alternative to fizzy drinks.

SNEAKING IN VEGGIES

Q *'The parents have asked me to make sure their child eats his vegetables, but he just won't. What should I do?'*

A Be a sneak. Although honesty's usually the best policy, Junior doesn't need to know that you've grated a little carrot into his meat loaf, hamburger or muffin mix, tossed a few tiny bits of cauliflower into his mac 'n' cheese or stirred some broccoli into his pasta dish (especially if it's covered up with plenty of tomato sauce). Or try making veggies more fun with a dip and serve them as an appetizer before lunch or dinner (so he'll be hungrier and more likely to tuck in). Remember, too, that nutritious fruits can match vegetables vitamin for vitamin.

a happy kitchen

Having trouble at the table? Whip up some fun dishes that are sure to be lunchtime winners.

Green Eggs and Ham

• • • • • • • • • • • • • • • • •

What's sillier than eating what you're reading about? After a session with the legendary Dr. Seuss book, enlist the child's help in making, and then eating, this great dish. (Even a child who usually turns up his nose at anything green will delight in green eggs.)

2 eggs
⅛ cup fresh parsley, chives or dill, minced
1 ounce turkey ham, cubed
Vegetable oil cooking spray, or 1 teaspoon butter or margarine

Beat the eggs. Add the herbs and ham. Grease a small skillet. Pour in egg mixture and cook over medium heat, mixing often, until eggs are set and no longer runny.

Serves 1 or 2

Egg in a Hole

• • • • • • • • • • • • • • • • • •

A twist on the classic sunny-side-up fried egg.

2 eggs
2 slices whole-wheat bread
Vegetable oil cooking spray,
or 1 teaspoon butter
or margarine

Using a round cookie cutter or the rim of a small glass, cut out a circle in the center of each slice of bread. Grease a medium skillet and place over medium heat. Put the bread slices and the cutout centres into the pan. Crack an egg into the centre opening of each slice of bread. Cook until the white part of the egg is set. Flip over the cutouts and the slices of bread and egg, and cook until the yolk is set. Serve the egg slices next to the circles, spread with the child's favourite jam. If you place a circle on top of each egg, you can call this dish 'Eggs with Hats On'.

Serves 1 or 2

Strawberry French Toast Fingers

• • • • • • • • • • • • • • • • • •

What young child wouldn't love to get his hands on these yummy fingers?

2 eggs
¼ cup milk
½ cup whole-fruit strawberry
preserve
8 slices whole-wheat bread,
crusts trimmed
Vegetable oil cooking spray,
or 1 teaspoon butter
or margarine

Beat the eggs with the milk. Spread the preserve onto four slices of bread. Top with the other four slices. Cut each sandwich into three strips. Dip each strip into the egg-milk mixture, making sure both sides are coated. Fry the strips in a greased skillet over medium heat until golden brown, turning them over as needed.

Serves 4

Muffin Pizza

• • • • • • • • • • • • • • • • •

Why order a takeaway when you can make these delicious pizzas at home?

3 whole-wheat muffins, split
3 ounces tomato sauce
3 ounces mozzarella cheese, shredded
Optional toppings: sliced mushrooms, sliced black olives, chopped tomatoes, sliced green peppers, small pieces of steamed broccoli

Preheat oven to 350°F. Place the muffin halves on an ungreased baking sheet. Spread each half with sauce and top with cheese. Add additional toppings if desired. Bake for 7 to 10 minutes, or until cheese is bubbly.

Serves 3 or 4

Crispy Chicken Nuggets

• • • • • • • • • • • • • • • • •

Serve up a bucket of these (or at least a plateful), and your young charge will do the chicken dance!

2 boneless, skinless chicken breasts, cut into bite-size pieces
1 egg, beaten
½ cup bread crumbs
½ cup grated Parmesan cheese
1 teaspoon butter

Preheat oven to 350°F. Combine bread crumbs and cheese. Dip each chicken piece into the egg, then into the bread crumb mixture, coating on all sides. Place chicken nuggets in a buttered shallow baking pan. Bake uncovered for approximately 30 minutes, until chicken is no longer pink inside. Serve with a tomato sauce for dipping.

Serves 2 or 3

playing

Child's play might seem like all fun and games to you, but to babies and young children it's much, much more. Playing is how children practise and perfect motor skills, how they discover the world around them, how they master concepts such as cause and effect. In other words, playing is the way children learn, which means it's never a waste of time. The more children play, the more they grow intellectually, physically and socially. So let the fun and games begin!

newborn to 6 months

GAMES TO PLAY

Babies under six months don't need much in the way of entertainment. Here are some games baby will love to play.

UNDER THREE MONTHS OLD. Offer the baby any of the following, but make sure all are safe for his age (no strings longer than six inches; no small pieces that might be chewed):

■ Rattles (attached to the baby's wrist or ankle, or put in his clenched fist to hold)

■ Soft, washable animals, dolls or balls

■ Toys that squeak when squeezed

■ Objects that are brightly coloured or have bold patterns (they're the easiest for baby to see)

■ A mobile (with or without music) attached to the crib rail (kept out of baby's reach for safety)

■ An unbreakable mirror (babies find their own reflections fascinating, even though they have no idea what they're looking at)

■ Soft books with easy-to-see patterns or decorations

■ Wind chimes hung close by (baby will love to listen to the sound and watch them move)

Ways to interact with baby:

■ Hold, rock, sing, coo and talk to the baby.

■ Play different kinds of music.

■ Make funny faces and funny noises.

■ Blow 'raspberries' or loud kisses on the baby's belly.

■ Play 'This Little Piggy' with baby (see page 78).

THREE TO SIX MONTHS OLD. Add on any of these toys at playtime (again, making sure all are safe):

■ Cloth, plastic or board books with large pictures

tummy time

SAFE AND SOUND

Though a baby must always be put to sleep on his back to reduce the chances of SIDS (sudden infant death syndrome), he must also have supervised tummy time if he is to learn how to lift that big head up (a necessary first step for rolling over, sitting, crawling and other tricks of the baby trade). That means you should put him down on his stomach at least once or twice a day. Be sure to stay close by, not only for safety's sake but to help him practice those new tricks.

- Large play blocks of wood or plastic
- Large plastic keys or rings
- Toys that roll
- Activity bars
- Floor mat and activity gym
- Toys that move and make noise
- Teething toys
- Musical toys

Ways to interact with baby:

- Play all kinds of music.
- Stick your tongue out, and watch baby copy you. Try smiling, closing your eyes and making simple sounds, too. Babies love to imitate.

- Bring baby to the window and point out all the exciting things that are going on outside.
- Copy any sound baby makes. He may continue making the sound to keep the game going.
- Put some chair cushions on the floor and let baby bounce and roll on them – always keeping your eyes and a hand on her while she's bouncing.
- Read books with lots of colour.
- Move baby's arms and legs in rhythm while you sing a song.
- Play peekaboo. Hide your face behind your hands and say, 'Where's (baby's name)?' Then take them away and say, 'Peekaboo!'

A PLACE TO PLAY

All young babies need for a good time is a loving care provider and a few toys. But if the parents have the following equipment on hand, feel free to use them with care.

PLAYPEN. For those times when you need to keep the baby out of harm's way for a few minutes (the phone just rang, you have to use the toilet, you need to mop up spilled formula), a playpen can come in very handy. With a few safe toys for company (a crib mirror or busy box, for instance), many babies will play happily for as long as 10 to 15 minutes before calling for some more personal attention. Even so, check on the baby often, never leave her in the playpen for longer than 20 minutes and never leave her alone on her tummy.

STATIONARY 'WALKERS'. Stationary 'walkers' that let a baby bounce, jump, spin and play while staying safely in one place, should be used only when you need to keep him safely seated for 10 to 15 minutes – and only when you're in the room with him.

Walkers that allow a baby to get around allow him to get into serious trouble, too. If the parents use such a walker, make

swing fling

SAFE AND SOUND

Keep these very important safety tips in mind whenever you put the baby in the swing:

■ Always carefully strap him into the swing.

■ Don't leave him alone in a room while he's swinging.

■ Make sure he can't grab anything from the swing that could hurt him.

■ Be sure his feet can't reach anything he might be able to push off from.

sure you don't leave the baby's side for *even a second* while he's in it.

SWING. Limit swing time to no longer than 15 minutes, and keep talking and playing with the baby as she swings (this isn't a substitute sitter). Also, be sure to move her to the cot before she dozes off.

TIMING PLAYTIME

Q *'There are many times during the day when the baby is sitting in an infant seat or lying on the rug – quiet and seemingly happy. Is that a good time to play, or should I leave her be?'*

A Actually, the best time to play with a baby is when she's quiet and happy (also known as her 'quiet alert' state). That's when she's most ready and eager for some one-on-one socializing, and best able to focus on an activity (whether it's a back-and-forth cooing session or a game of peekaboo). On the other hand, a baby who seems happy but whose motor is running (she's making small sounds, her arms moving and legs kicking) is more interested in taking in the big picture than doing one-on-

one time. She'll like watching you bustle around with your chores, but she won't be able to concentrate on play. That's the best time for you to take care of other business (with her safe and within eyeshot), but be sure to swoop down her way now and then for a little interaction on the run.

Something else to keep in mind: If you wait for the baby to become fussy before playing with her, you'll never get any really good playing done. Fussy babies are definitely not in the mood for fun and games.

BABY TALK

Feel silly talking to a baby who can't understand a word you're saying? Don't. Babies who are talked to early and often learn language faster. They also feel loved and appreciated ('What I have to say matters!'). So anytime you're together and the baby is alert enough to pay attention, talk it up. For example:

- Give baby a play-by-play as you change his nappy.

- Offer cooking lessons as you make his formula.

■ Ask his opinion as you decide whether to buy carrots or cucumbers.

■ Sing silly songs and recite rhymes (see pages 78–79 for some suggestions).

■ Match him coo for coo. If he says 'ah-oo', say 'ah-oo' right back.

■ Switch between baby talk ('That's yummy for your tummy!') and grown-up talk ('That's delicious to eat!').

6 to 12 months

These days, baby is a barrel of laughs (and squeals and giggles) – making playtime more fun for both of you. Plus, as baby develops new skills (sitting, picking things up, crawling), you can play in more ways than ever before.

GAMES TO PLAY

Now that baby is more active and alert, games get her moving, exploring, thinking and learning.

LET'S GET PHYSICAL . . . No couch potato (or tater tot) here. After spending the first six months in someone's arms, a stroller or an infant seat, it doesn't get more fun than rolling over, sitting, crawling and cruising. To help get baby moving, you can:

■ **Let'm out.** Keep baby's time in a stationary walker, swings, bouncy seats and pushchairs to a minimum, so he can practise those important physical skills.

■ **Go for a change.** Until baby can change his own position, help him along, moving him from back to tummy, from propped up to lying down, from the crib or playpen to the floor.

■ **Do the jig.** Pull baby up to a standing position on your lap and encourage him to bounce.

■ **Help out.** When baby is still in the learning stages, you can:

  □ Gently pull her up to sitting.

  □ Sit her upright, propped up with pillows if necessary but always supervised.

  □ Get her into a crawling position. Give her lots and lots of chances to be on the floor (supervised, of course) so she can give crawling or creeping a shot.

■ **Make baby reach.** Place toys just out of his reach on the floor so he needs to creep or crawl to reach them. Cheer him on when he tries to inch forward (or backwards, which is how many babies start crawling).

■ **Cruise control.** Encourage a baby who has started cruising by arranging the furniture so she can move (safely) across the room.

■ **Be pushy.** Offer push toys to help baby stay steady as he takes those first tentative steps.

■ **Don't hold back.** Once baby can walk, let her walk as much as possible – to the park, to the postbox, down the hall. Yes, there will be a lot of falls (so stay close). Yes, walking with her will take forever. But it's a skill that takes practice, practice, practice for her – and patience, patience, patience for the adults in her life.

■ **Get out of the house!** Go to the park, the museum, the bookshop, the toy store, the playground, into the garden, the

take a toy test

SAFE AND SOUND

Even toys that appear safe may be dangerous – especially if they have small parts that can be pulled off. Any toy (or removable parts of a toy) or other object that can easily fit through a toilet-paper tube is too small for a child under three years old.

shopping mall, or other busy or exciting places where baby can walk and crawl in a new environment (always safely supervised).

LET'S GET GRABBY . . . Moving those arms and legs is important, but fingers (and that brain!) also need a workout. Encourage the development of fine motor skills by helping the baby play with any of these:

- Push and pull toys
- Activity boards
- Blocks
- Shape sorters
- Stacking toys
- Large Lego (babies can choke on small ones)
- Nontoxic crayons and paper (though make sure the baby doesn't start munching on those yummy-looking crayons)
- Buckets and sand or water
- Floating bath toys
- Large and small stuffed animals to hug and hold

- Household objects (real or toy), such as telephones (cordless), mixing spoons, measuring cups, strainers, pots and pans, paper cups, empty boxes
- Small riding toys
- Balls of all sorts

Those little hands will also love getting into the action when you play hand game favourites like peekaboo, pat-a-cake and follow the leader (you start clapping, then encourage baby to copy).

JOINING IN THE FUN

Q *'I love playing with the baby, but sometimes I wonder if I'm doing all I can to make playtime stimulating enough for her.'*

A The first thing to remember is that babies learn best through life's simplest interactions – the kinds of things you're probably already doing without even thinking about it. They learn by looking out a window (while being held safely in your arms) and watching a fire engine zoom past. By filling up and dumping a cup of water in the tub. By watching you disappear behind a sofa ('Peekaboo'), then pop up again ('I see you!'). By banging on pots and pans on the kitchen floor. Second, babies learn best when they're encouraged. So when you're playing together, be more than a pal – be a cheerleader. Clap when the baby puts a shape in the right slot or starts barking when she sees a puppy in the park.

MESSY PLAYTIME

Q *'It's no surprise that the 10-month-old baby I care for makes a big mess every time he plays. Should I expect him to help me clean it up?'*

A It's way too early to expect neatness – but it's never too early to begin teaching it. Start by showing him how it's done. He'll love copying you as you put blocks back into a box or toys onto the shelf. In fact, if you make cleanup part of the play, he'll even come to look forward to it. Sing cleanup songs ('This is the way we clean our toys, clean our toys, clean our toys . . .') and, as he gets older, use the other suggestions you'll find on page 90.

Don't get carried away with neatness, though. Making a mess is part of the fun and part of the learning process. For instance, when the baby dumps the blocks out on the floor (even if you just put them neatly back into the bin), he's learning about cause and effect, about empty and full. Give him plenty of chances to get down and dirty, too (within safety limits, of course). Babies (and just about everything in their path) are washable.

BABY TALK

Babies aren't born knowing the language. But by the second half of the first year, they start to pick up a word or two . . . and then 10 . . . and then more. Understanding will come first, followed soon by those first spoken words. And they learn it all by listening to the adults around them – like you. Here are some ways to get baby understanding and talking:

GO SLOW. Speak slowly, clearly and simply.

LABEL, LABEL, LABEL. Tell baby what everything is called. Point out the bottle, the toys, the stove, the hat, the fire truck, the police officer, the squirrel, the trees and his favourite – the other babies.

SAY IT AGAIN. When talking to baby, pick out one word to say again and again: 'I'm pouring baby some milk' . . . 'Sophia likes milk' . . . 'Milk tastes good' . . . 'Here comes the milk'.

TALK CONCEPTS. In the bath, discuss the difference between *hot* and *cold*. On the stairs, point out *up* and *down*. Talk about *wet* and *dry* while changing a nappy, *big* and *little* when playing with an older sister, *inside* and *outside* when going indoors or leaving for a trip to the park or playground.

STICK WITH NAMES. *Her, my, he, it, we* and *they* are confusing for babies. Use names instead: 'This is Sam's doll.' 'Where are Mummy's books?'

REPEAT AFTER BABY. When baby tries to talk (or more likely babble), repeat what she says. If baby says 'ba-ba-ba', repeat 'ba-ba-ba' (even if it makes you feel like a sheep). When she says 'mmm-mmm', you say 'mmmmm'. See what happens when you add your own sound, such as 'da-da-da'. She might surprise you one day and repeat after you!

LISTEN UP. When baby talks to you, answer back (even if you have no idea what you're agreeing to). This lets baby know that people talk to each other. If baby babbles 'oh-ga-ba', counter with 'Oh, you don't say' or 'Is that so?' When he's clearly asking for something, work together to figure out what it is. 'Do you want the ball? Do you want the cup?' It will be frustrating, but before you know it, he'll be saying 'ball' and 'cup'.

SING ALONG. Singing songs with rhymes helps babies learn and enjoy sounds. Check out the great rhyming songs on pages 78–79.

READ OVER AND OVER. It's never too early to read to a baby: simple rhyming books with colourful pictures, board books with pictures of babies, Dr Seuss. And don't forget to label as you read. Point to the dog on the page as you say 'dog'. Soon you'll be able to ask 'Where is the dog?' and watch baby point it out.

GIVE DIRECTIONS. Tell baby to 'wave bye-bye to the girl, please' or 'please give Daddy his keys' while showing what those directions mean (wave bye-bye to the girl, give Daddy his keys). Soon, baby will be able to do it herself.

TALK LIKE A GROWN-UP. Leave the baby talk to the baby. Using simple adult words will help him learn to talk faster (though adding a 'y' to the end of some words – 'doggy' or 'kitty' – to make them more appealing to baby ears is fine). So call a bottle a bottle, not a baba. When the baby starts using baby talk, don't criticize. But do help him make the connection to the grown-up forms of the words. For instance, when he says 'da' at the sight of the neighbour's poodle, say, 'That's right – dog!'

A SECOND LANGUAGE

Q *'I speak English, but Spanish is my first language. Would it be okay for me to teach some Spanish phrases to the children I care for?'*

A Many parents would welcome the opportunity for their child to learn another language, especially from a native speaker. And learning a second language will never be easier or more natural than when you're very young (and still learning your own language). Young minds are sponges for just about everything, and they soak up new words and grammar much more quickly than adults or older children do. Early exposure to a second language also helps children learn other languages more easily later on.

Still, before you begin the Spanish lessons, check with the parents. If they're on board with the idea, ask them how they'd like you to go about it. There are several options: you could speak a combination of English and Spanish to the children, speak only Spanish (they'll probably learn the language faster this way) or speak in English but read stories and sing songs in Spanish.

MUSIC TO BABY'S EARS

Can't remember those songs your mum used to sing to you, or those rhymes she used to recite? Here are some of the old baby favourites that have been passed down from nursery to nursery:

IF YOU'RE HAPPY. Sing 'If you're happy and you know it, clap your hands,' and show baby how to clap. Soon he'll learn how to clap on his own. Try clapping feet, too, for a change of pace.

THIS LITTLE PIGGY WENT TO MARKET. Wiggle each toe as you recite 'This little piggy went to market, this little piggy stayed home, this little piggy had roast beef, this little piggy had none, and this little piggy went "wee, wee, wee, wee, wee" – all the way home.' Walk your fingers from baby's toes to her tummy or chin as you say 'wee, wee, wee, wee'. End with a loud kiss.

SO BIG. Ask 'How big is baby?' (or use his name, the dog's name or a sibling's name), help him to spread his arms as wide as possible, and then exclaim excitedly 'So big!'

INCEY WINCEY SPIDER. While using hand movements to act out the lyrics, sing, 'Incey Wincey spider climed up the water spout, down came the rain and washed the spider out, out came the sunshine and dried up all the rain, and Incey Wincey spider went up the spout again.'

EYES, NOSE, MOUTH. Take the baby's hands in yours, touch one to each of your eyes, then both to your nose, then to your mouth (where you end with a kiss), naming each feature as you move along: 'Eyes, nose, mouth, kiss.' Nothing teaches these names faster.

RING AROUND THE ROSES. Once baby is walking, hold hands in a circle, sing 'Ring a-ring o' roses, a pocket full of posies, A-tishoo! A-tishoo! We all fall down' and end with a fall to the floor. You can also play this one with the baby in your arms (just be gentle as you fall down).

ONE, TWO, BUCKLE MY SHOE. Recite 'One, two, buckle my shoe; three, four, shut the door; five, six, pick up sticks; seven, eight, lay them straight; nine, ten, start again' to teach baby counting.

POP GOES THE WEASEL. Sit the baby on your lap and sing, 'Half a pound of tuppenny rice, half a pound of treacle. That's the way the money goes . . .' and then, 'popping' the baby into a standing position, finish with 'Pop goes the weasel!' Once baby knows the song really well, wait a few moments after you say 'pop' – to give him a chance to do the popping!

READING TO BABY

Q *'The parents want me to read a book or two each day to their 10-month-old. I know he doesn't understand what I'm reading to him – and sometimes he won't stay on my lap for the entire time. Why should I even bother?'*

A Although the baby will probably spend more time chewing on books than listening to them at this age, it's never too soon to start the reading habit. Before his first birthday, he'll begin to pay attention to the words (not for their meaning, but for their rhythm and sound) and the illustrations (enjoying the colour and patterns before he understands what they represent). By reading to him from an early age, you'll be encouraging a love of books – and giving him a head start on learning.

1 to 3 years

If play is the business of childhood (which it is), it's time to get down to business. For toddlers, play is fun, plus the way to learn and practise social skills.

GAMES TO PLAY

So many things for toddlers to do, so few hours in the day. Let's get playing!

LET'S GET PHYSICAL. Toddlers need to move to develop their muscles, to use up some of that endless energy (so they can eat and sleep better) and to continue to grow well. You may be more tired out at the end of a play session than they are, but be sure to get them:

■ Swinging on a swing

■ Sliding down a slide

■ Cutting paper (with safety scissors and supervision)

■ Pounding play dough

■ Rolling cookie dough

■ Dancing

■ Running races

■ Playing ball

■ Pulling wagons

■ Hopping, skipping and jumping

■ Playing on riding toys

LET'S GET IMAGINATIVE. With a little imagination, a child can be a firefighter, a doctor, a mum or dad, or a pilot (even the sky's not the limit). Children can also use imaginative play to work out feelings and fears:

■ Make believe (pretending he's a daddy and you're a baby, or she's a doctor and you're a sick patient; cooking pretend food in a play kitchen and serving it to you in a pretend restaurant). Add dolls and teddy bears to the cast, too.

■ Dressing up. Ask Dad for some old shirts, Mum for some hats and handbags, or pull together some costumes yourself.

■ Make up stories and tell them together. Ask, 'What do you think will happen next?'

LET'S GET CREATIVE. Anything that allows a toddler to get creative will also help him learn.

■ Painting and finger painting

■ Drawing with crayons

■ Making collages

■ Building with blocks

- Humming or singing songs

- Playing 'follow the leader'

- Beating a drum or 'playing' other musical instruments

- Playing with sand

- Playing with water

- Shaping play dough

LET'S GET SMART. Allowing toddlers to explore the world around them not only helps them learn but nurtures the little scientists inside them. Collecting leaves as they fall off the tree, pointing out different-colour cars, finding out that muffins rise in the oven or that big containers hold more water than small ones, watching the snow pile up by the inches, observing a squirrel gather nuts – there's no end to the possibilities for learning when you're with a toddler.

LET'S GET SOCIAL. Toddlers will begin to relate to other children by touching them, watching them, speaking to them – and sometimes even playing with them.

GAME GUIDELINES

Keep these guidelines in mind when you start playing with a toddler:

UNPLUG THE TV. Educational television may have some value, but toddlers learn a lot more from doing than from watching. Be strict about enforcing limits that the parents have placed on TV (and computer) use, and play games instead. (See page 87 for more on toddlers and TV.)

GET OUT OF THE HOUSE. Spend some time outside each day – in the garden, at the playground, a park, a football field. Toddlers need fresh air and a chance to play outdoors, even on cold days.

JOIN IN THE FUN. Don't just sit and watch a toddler play. Challenge her to a round of hide-and-seek or a game of catch. Draw or build block cities together. Play teddy bear hospital, supermarket or house. But don't butt into every game a toddler plays. It's good for a child to learn how to play by herself sometimes, too.

LET THERE BE A MESS. It's okay for kids to get messy (within reason, of course). Put on a smock and let the toddler squish the finger paints between his fingers. Don't worry if he rolls in the grass – those stains will come out in the wash and bath.

DON'T BE A CRITIC. Find something to praise in the child's artwork, even if she's coloured outside the lines or you can't tell which side is up. Tell her how fine her Lego castle looks even if it looks more like a tornado-flattened barn. But also ask what she likes about the work, so she doesn't become too dependent on your praise.

MAKE CLEAN-UP A GAME. Clean-up time can be almost as much fun as playtime. (See page 90.)

PLAYING WITH FRIENDS

Put two toddlers in a room, and they'll probably ignore each other. And when that gets boring, they'll fight over the same doll's pram, have a tug-of-war over a truck, pull hair, push, pinch . . . you get the picture. To bring out the best in toddler play sessions:

BE THERE. A toddler is too young to be left alone at someone else's house to play. Even if the toddler seems ready (has no separation anxiety, plays nicely, and so on), it's a lot for one adult to be left in

---

TRICKS OF THE TRADE

the art of cleaning up

Spread old newspaper before starting an art project. Then, when the masterpiece is finished, all you have to do is roll the mess up in the newspaper and dump it.

when playtime is over

Most children might have a hard time putting their toys down. To make it easier, you may want to:

TRICKS OF THE TRADE

■ **START THE WARNING CLOCK.** Say, 'It's almost time to stop for lunch.' Then, 'In five minutes it will be lunchtime.' Finally, 'Okay, it's time to eat.' Or set a buzzer to signal that playtime is over.

■ **FINISH UP.** If the child is working on a painting or a block tower, let him put the finishing touches on it before you make him put it away.

■ **STRIKE A BARGAIN.** If she's playing with a doll, suggest that the doll come with you to the supermarket.

■ **BE PATIENT – but only to a point.** Eventually you may have to gently but firmly end the activity, pick up the toddler and carry him to dinner (blow big raspberries on his belly, and he might forget to protest).

charge of two toddlers (isn't one hard enough sometimes?).

STAY NEUTRAL. Toddlers rarely share nicely (which is perfectly normal). You'll have fewer fights over toys if you arrange play times in neutral places like the park, the library or a playground.

BRING TOYS FROM HOME. If the play session is at someone else's house, bring along a few of the

toddler's favourite toys to make sharing less difficult.

KEEP IT SHORT. Long play times can lead to meltdowns, so keep them under two hours (and well under that for one-year-olds).

TIME IT RIGHT. If you're setting the time, plan play sessions around nap and feeding schedules so the toddler is well fed and rested before visiting or hosting.

DON'T OVERSCHEDULE. If you're making the arrangements, keep in mind that more than one or two play times a week can be too much for even the most social of toddlers. All that sharing and playing nicely can be stressful and can lead to burnout. Besides, toddlers need downtime – it's hard always being 'on.'

THE OTHER SITTER

Q *'My employers are constantly arranging play sessions with their best friend's son, but I really don't get along with his nanny. What should I do?'*

A Try to be a sport; after all, it's more important for the children to get along than it is for the nannies. It may help to look for something positive in the other nanny's personality (there has to be something!), or just keep the conversation light and limited (and when she starts getting under your skin, just smile, nod and turn your attention to the kids).

Do bring the subject up with the parents, though, if these occasions are truly unbearable for you (chances are the child will sense your feelings and be unhappy, too).

Ask them if you can schedule at least some play times with nannies of your choosing.

PLAYGROUP BASICS

During the toddler years, playgroups become a great way for children to learn how to play together and make friends. If the parents have arranged for you and their toddler to attend a playgroup, enjoy! If they haven't, but wouldn't mind if you did, consider joining one. After all, no matter how much you love caring for children, it's also fun to spend some time with people who speak in full sentences and don't need help with the potty. Alternatively, you might consider setting up a group with other carers and/or parents. If so, here are some tips on getting going:

CHOOSE A NUMBER. No more than five very young toddlers should get together at a time. Older toddlers can usually handle as many as 10 regular members in their group (particularly since one or two kids are bound to be at home sick during each session). Children in the same playgroup tend to get along better if they're all within about four or five months of one another in age.

STICK TO A SCHEDULE. Playgroups work best if they meet at the same time on the same day each week. Either hire a hall or rotate homes so that everyone gets a chance to be a host – and a guest.

PLAY BY THE RULES. Each group needs to decide on some rules, concerning health (sick children shouldn't come to playgroup), supervision (how many adults will always be in the room) and food (which snacks are appropriate and which are not, especially if any of the children in the group have allergies).

WATCH BUT DON'T HOVER. Keep an eye on the kids, but don't get in the way of their play. (Step in to break up a fight, however, before blocks – and fists – start flying.)

PLAN ACTIVITIES. Too much free play – as important as it is – may lead to a free-for-all fight over toys. When that happens, have an adult-supervised group activity (such as finger painting) ready to go.

Q 'At playgroup last week, another parent – who happens to be a friend of the parents I work for – asked if I would come work for her. I said no, of course, but I'm not sure whether I should tell my employers.'

A It's never a good idea to keep secrets from your employers, even if you're trying to protect their friend or their friendship. During your next meeting, mention what happened and let them know that you said no to the other parent but that the offer made you uncomfortable. Hopefully, they'll bring it up with their friend so it doesn't happen again.

TALK IT UP

A toddler has come a long, long way in the communication department, but there's still so much more to learn. There are plenty of fun ways to talk to toddlers so they'll talk to you.

PLAY ASKING GAMES. What colour is the sky? Why is that girl happy? What sound do dogs make?

PLAY WORD GAMES. While you're reading a book together, point to the pictures and ask, 'What is that animal?' or 'Do you know the name of that fruit?'

PLAY THE ALPHABET GAME. As the toddler gets older, point out letters. 'There's a C for cat. There's an R for rainbow.' Then get personal: 'R is also for Rachel!'

POINT OUT SIGNS. Show the toddler a stop sign, an exit sign, a one-way sign. Read what signs say as you pass them.

PLAY 'I SPY'. This old favourite teaches language like no other. Begin by saying 'I spy with my little eye' and follow up with 'something that's blue' or 'something that starts with B.' Then have the toddler guess what you're looking at.

TEACH SHAPES. Circles, squares and triangles are everywhere –

in that sandwich, that pizza, that sign. Point them out, and ask for help finding more.

COUNT. When you walk up the stairs or give out crackers, count them aloud.

SPELL. Show an older toddler how to spell her name. Talk about names for things that start with each letter.

THE SAME OLD STORY

Q *'The child I mind wants to do the same things the same way every single day. He even wants me to read from the same book. Won't he get bored?'*

A Because toddlers are growing and changing so quickly, they get a lot of comfort from consistency: the orange juice always served in the blue cup; the bedtime routine that always includes the same three stories (read in the same order); the favourite tattered blanket that's always there to cling to; listening to the same songs; and playing the same games over and over again. Since they're ready for an encore long after you're bored, be a good sport and play it again!

TV AND TODDLERS

Chances are, the parents will set limits on TV watching (so the toddler doesn't watch the day away). Follow the rules they've established for their household, but also keep these viewing tips in mind:

WATCH TOGETHER. Don't plop a toddler in front of the TV just so you can do something else. Make the viewing interactive. Ask questions about the action ('Where do you think that little girl is going?') and talk about the show ('Isn't Cookie Monster being silly?').

KEEP THE SHOW GOING – not by watching it longer, but by doing activities or reading books that connect to the programme. If a TV show was about friendship, read a book about friends when the show is over. If *Sesame Street* introduced the number three, count three steps to the bathtub, three slices of pear at snack, three chicken fingers at dinner, and so on.

DON'T OFFER TV AS A BRIBE. Linking television with good behaviour (or taking it away as a punishment) will only make it more attractive.

TURN IT OFF. Avoid using the TV as a background to other activities – and don't watch it yourself while the toddler is doing something else.

TV LIMITS

Q *'Even though the mother has decided her child can watch only one TV show per day, I find it very hard not to give in when the child asks if he can watch just one more programme.'*

A Nothing is more important in child-rearing than consistency – and that means enforcing the house rules consistently, even if you don't always agree with them (or if they're hard to follow). Not only will the child be more secure if you stick to the rules (it's confusing when the rules are always negotiable or changing), but your relationship with your employer will be more secure, too. Stick to the one-show-a-day rule.

4 to 6 years

GAMES TO PLAY

With all those new skills to use, and so many games and activities to choose from, four- to six-year-olds should never be bored.

LET'S GET PHYSICAL. From bike riding to roller-skating to ball-playing, there's almost nothing that this age group can't do or won't try. Make sure the child gets some physical activity every day.

LET'S GET DRAMATIC. Children this age love to play dressing up and put on 'shows'. Rummage in the dressing up trunk, make some costumes out of paper, boxes or fabric scraps, or use the power of make-believe to set the stage.

LET'S GET MUSICAL. Put on some music and play a game of musical statues (everyone freezes when the music stops). Give out children's instruments – a drum, a triangle or maybe a xylophone – and create a band.

LET'S GET CREATIVE. Encourage the child to plot out a building on paper and then construct the building out of blocks, Lego or other kid-sized building equipment. Put out paints or crayons, and tape a giant piece of paper on the floor so the child can create a mural. Make sculptures with papier-mâché or clay, puppets out of paper bags or socks, or necklaces with cereal or beads and string. And don't forget that favourite – the collage. Armed with paste, paper, dried leaves, cutouts from magazines, dried macaroni – you name it – there's no end to what he can craft.

LET'S GET SMART. No chance of being bored when there are board games around. But to avoid frustration, make sure the game is age- and skill-appropriate before putting it out.

LET'S PLAY NICELY TOGETHER

An infant-school child has come a long way since her days of hair-pulling and biting (hopefully). But they still have many social lessons to learn – from how to play games fairly to how to disagree nicely. Each little (and big) fight they have with their friends is a chance to learn one of those lessons. You can help by:

STEPPING IN. A four- or five-year-old knows how to pick a fight, but doesn't yet know how to settle one. You'll need to offer simple, specific guidelines for working out any disputes the child has with his friends. He needs to learn that taking turns is fair, whether it's about what game to play or who gets to go first. He also needs to learn that it's okay to disagree, but not to yell or use force (like pulling a toy out of his friend's hand).

BEING THERE. Prevention is always better than reaction. Look for situations that are likely to start a fight, such as a particular game or toy, and redirect the children to an activity that's less likely to create conflict.

PRAISING. A little positive reinforcement goes a long way. When you see the child playing nicely with her friend, praise her both at the time and afterwards.

SETTING A POSITIVE EXAMPLE.
Read books that show children cooperating and playing together nicely.

SAY NO TO ABUSE

Q *'At playgroup today, I saw a nannny hit the child she takes care of. Should I say something? To whom?'*

A Most of the time, the other caregivers you'll meet will be wonderful, warm and devoted professionals. But if you ever see another childminder hit a child, or let a child wander off in the playground while she chats with her friends, let your employer or the other carer's employer know. If you see a childcarer leave a child alone in the park or otherwise put that child in serious danger, call your employer or the police immediately. Getting involved can keep a child from being harmed.

PLAY DATE CLEANUP

Q *'A child who comes over to play always makes a terrible mess and never helps to clean up. I don't think it's fair, but I don't know what to do.'*

A This age group is old enough to clean up its own mess, but not yet old enough to remember to do it without being told. For best results – and to make clean-up an activity that kids actually look forward to – bring on the fun. Make clean-up a contest ('Who can put more blocks in the box?'), set the clean-up to music (fast cleaning when the music is fast, slower cleaning when the music is slow) or set a timer and have the children race to see if they can beat the clock. This way, the clean-up becomes an enjoyable part of the play session and you're left with a clean house after the others leave.

READY FOR READING

A lthough many five- or six-year-olds may already be reading and writing, some are pre-readers. You can help by encouraging the reader-to-be.

MAKE READING A ROUTINE.
Read to the child every day. Set aside a regular reading time (at bedtime or right after school, for instance), but also read whenever it seems appropriate (when

he's bored with a game, when he needs a little downtime, when he's wired and needs to unwind, and so on). There's never a bad time for reading (except during meals, which should be a time for talking). And remember, even children who can read to themselves enjoy – and benefit from – being read to.

KEEP BOOKS IN REACH. Leave books where the child can find them (on low shelves or in baskets on the floor). Children will naturally pick up books and 'read' (making up stories to go with the pictures, reciting from books they know by heart and, in time, trying to sound out words).

VISIT THE LIBRARY. If there's a library nearby, use your card (or ask the parents if they have one) so you and the child can borrow books together. That way, there will always be something new to read. Many libraries have story hours, too. (So do bookshops; check those out also.)

FIND BOOKS THAT FIT. If the child loves fire trucks, read books about firefighters and fire engines. If it's Barney that tickles the child purple, read Barney books.

TALK AS YOU READ. Even before children are ready to read, they're ready to dig deeper into stories. Ask questions as you read: 'What do you think Madeline will do next?' or 'What's Harold doing in the picture?'

READ WHEREVER YOU ARE. Show the child that reading is an important part of everyday life. Read shop signs as you walk to school, read labels in the market, spell out the letters on a stop sign ('S-T-O-P spells *stop*') on your way to the park.

LISTEN TO BOOKS ON TAPE. The library will have audio versions of books to check out – or ask the parents if they can pick some up at a bookshop. Children love listening to someone else tell a story, and they can follow along in their own books.

computer bytes

SAFE AND SOUND

Even if you don't know a mouse from a modem, chances are an infant-school child does. Children as young as two and three are using computers these days. Ask the parents what their guidelines are for computer use. How much time can the child spend on the computer each day? Which games can he play? Does he have access to the Internet and, if so, does he need supervision when he's online – even if parental controls are in place?

MAKE READING PART OF PLAY. Some ideas include:

■ Combine reading with the child's love of dressing-up to bring a book to life. Have him dress up like a character in his favourite story and act it out.

■ Put on a puppet show. Make your own puppets from paper bags or old socks, or use ones the child already has to tell a story from a book.

■ Cut out pictures from magazines and help the child arrange them by letter (A is for apple, D is for dog). Then make an alphabet book by gluing the pictures onto paper.

■ Instead of reading a book, sing it to the child's favourite tune. Put on a silly voice and really make it fun.

■ Encourage the child to 'write' her own book by drawing pictures and telling you what the story is. You can write down the words, and the child can show it to her parents.

TV TIME

It's hard to keep this age group and TV apart altogether. After all, even if a child is allowed little TV watching in his home, he may get plenty of it when he visits other homes. Still, since there are so many better (and healthier) ways for a child to pass the time than sitting in front of a screen, always think before turning on the tube.

FOLLOW LIMITS. Allow the child to watch only as much TV as the parents' rules permit. Set a timer so the child knows when TV time is up.

VIEW WITH CARE. Shows that contain violence, sex, drug use or even frightening current events are not right for young children – even if they're cartoons that are marketed as 'children's programmes'. Ask the parents for guidelines on what their child can and can't watch. Then follow them.

WATCH TOGETHER. Explain the difference between a programme and an advert (where many advertisers are just trying to get children to ask for things they don't really need) and between real and make-believe (big yellow birds don't really talk).

VIEW VIDEOS. DVDs and videos have two advantages. One, you (and the parents) will know exactly what the child is watching. Two, there are no adverts (although that's also an advantage of the BBC of course).

RAINY-DAY ACTIVITIES

Too wet or cold for a trip to the playground? You can cure cabin fever fast with these ideas:

PLAY WITH DOUGH. A three-in-one fun fest – cooking, preparing, playing.

2 cups flour
4 teaspoons cream of tartar
1 cup salt
1½ to 2 cups boiling water
3 to 4 tablespoons vegetable oil
Food colouring (a few drops)

Let the child help you measure the ingredients (with the exception of the boiling water) before pouring them into a large bowl. Mix and knead the dough yourself until it cools, then let the child take over. Roll, pound, shape and flatten! And while you shouldn't encourage eating, don't worry if a few odds and ends find their way into the child's mouth – this dough's not toxic.

TRACE ME! Lay out sheets of newspaper or large white paper (taped together if necessary). Have the child lie down on the paper so you can trace his outline with a marker. Then let him 'colour himself in' and surprise the parents! You can do the same project using hands and feet. If you keep these drawings, a child can see how much bigger those outlines become as he grows.

TREASURE HUNTS. Hide small objects, such as blocks, toy cars or balls, around the house and send the child on a treasure hunt to see if she can find them.

KITCHEN CONCERT. Using pots, wooden spoons, small unbreakable bottles filled with pasta, beans or rice (tightly sealed) and other 'noisy' household objects, make a concert, have a parade, play musical statues.

CRAYON RUBBING. Find a flat bumpy object (a leaf, sandpaper, a piece of screen, a key, a penny), and place white paper over it. Remove the wrapper from a crayon, and gently rub the side of the crayon on the white paper.

MAGAZINE COLLAGE. Using old magazines (ask the parents for some or bring your own from home), cut out pictures (or if the child is old enough, allow her to do the cutting) and get the child to make a collage with paste and paper. Use nontoxic paste, or make your own as part of the fun: combine ¼ cup cornflour, ¾ cup water and 2 tablespoons corn syrup in a small pot over medium heat; stir until thick; remove from heat and let cool.

EDIBLE JEWELLERY. Cut a piece of wool to the length of a long (not tight) necklace or bracelet. Using cereal with holes in the centre, start by tying a piece of cereal to the end to keep all the cereal from falling off. Get the child to thread the wool through each piece of cereal. When finished, tie the ends together and let the child enjoy wearing and eating it! Be sure to make it big enough for the child to put it on and take it off easily, but don't let the child wear the necklace without supervision.

PAPER BAG PUPPETS. Use markers, crayons, felt, fabric, glitter, feathers, tissue paper and other craft supplies to make puppets out of paper lunch bags. Then put on a puppet show.

BOOKMARKS. Cut the two bottom corners off a stiff envelope to create bookmarks that will fit on the edge of a page. Decorate them – they make a great present for Mum or Dad.

PAPERWEIGHTS. Look for smooth, flat rocks in the park. Have the child decorate them with paint or glued-on items. Another great gift idea for Mum or Dad!

BUBBLES. A perennial outdoor favourite:

1 cup water
⅓ cup washing-up liquid
2 tablespoons light corn syrup

Combine ingredients, and blow bubbles using a standard bubble blower, a household item such as a potato masher, or a wire hanger bent into an interesting shape. Don't allow tasting, though.

◆ ◆ ◆

going out

being an in-home caregiver doesn't mean you'll be giving all your care in the home. Not by a long shot! Taking a baby or an older child out for some fresh air and exploration (whether it's for a stroll in the park, a spin around the supermarket, an afternoon at the art museum or a look-but-don't-buy browse through a toy shop) will be a welcome part of his day—and yours.

A little preparation will make any outing more fun (and less stressful). So get ready to get out!

newborn to 6 months

Babies are pretty portable, but getting them ready to go takes a little planning, a little organization, and a lot of packing.

WHAT BABY SHOULD WEAR

Fashion doesn't matter a bit when you're dressing baby for an outing, but comfort and safety always do.

IN COLD WEATHER. When the temperature tumbles, you'll need to keep the baby comfortably warm, but never hot. Dress her in several light layers (vest, outfit, cotton sweater, jacket or snowsuit and hat) so you can peel some off when you enter an overheated store or board a stuffy bus, or when the weather takes a turn for the warmer.

IN HOT WEATHER. The baby doesn't need to be dressed more warmly than you do in mild weather. In fact, overdressing the baby may cause overheating, which can be very dangerous. If it's a little windy or chilly in the morning, add a light sweater that you can take off when the weather heats up.

IN ALL WEATHER. Babies need extra protection for their heads. In cold or cool weather, they should always wear a hat (they lose a lot of heat through their heads). In hot, sunny weather, a wide-brimmed hat will shield the baby's head, face and eyes from the sun (and don't forget the baby-safe sunscreen).

DRESSING FOR SUCCESS

Q *'Sometimes I worry that the baby is either too hot or too cold when I take him outside. How can I be sure he's dressed right?'*

A Babies will often signal that they're uncomfortably cold or hot by fussing or crying. If you're unsure, use the back of your hand

ban the burn

SAFE AND SOUND

No sunbathing for baby. Young skin burns very easily, even when it's cold outside. So be sure to:

■ Always use a baby-safe sunscreen with an SPF over 45.

■ Put a hat with a wide brim on the baby's head in the summer.

■ Use pushchair umbrellas or sunshades to screen the baby from the sun's harmful rays.

■ When out and about, always look for the shady side of the street. Avoid spending too much time outside when the sun is at its strongest, between 11 A.M. and 4 P.M.

to check the back of his neck, arms or midsection. Feeling the baby's feet and hands won't tell you what you need to know, since they're usually cooler than the rest of his body.

If the baby feels cool, add another layer of clothing or a blanket, or bring him inside to a warm room. If he feels sweaty, take a layer off or bring him inside to a comfortably cool room.

A good rule of thumb: Dress the baby as you dress yourself (though his outfit will probably be cuter). If you're wearing three layers, he'll probably need three layers, too.

DON'T LEAVE HOME WITHOUT . . .

Babies don't travel light, even when they're just on a stroll through the park. That's where the nappy bag comes in handy. Stock it well when stepping out with baby, and don't leave home without:

A CHANGING PAD. If the nappy bag doesn't have a built-in waterproof pad, pack one to protect carpeting, beds or furniture when you're changing the baby during a visit or to turn a park bench into a makeshift changing table.

NAPPIES. Estimate how many the baby will need based on how long your outing will be – and then take at least one more.

BABY WIPES. Carry wipes in a small convenience pack (don't forget to refill it often) or in a small zip-lock plastic bag.

MUSLIN SQUARES. Nothing like smelly shoulders to cut short a nice day's outing.

ZIP-LOCK PLASTIC BAGS. When there's no rubbish bin in sight, or when you need to bring wet and soiled baby clothes home, these bags are lifesavers.

A MEAL. If you'll be out when it's time for a feed, you'll have to take a meal along. Don't forget the ice pack to keep bottles cold.

A CHANGE OF BABY CLOTHES. Between nappy leaks, spit-ups and spills, you'll want to bring an extra outfit (or two) wherever you go. It's amazing how many tops and bottoms a baby can go through in a day!

AN ADDITIONAL BLANKET OR SWEATER. In the spring and autumn, when temperatures often change without warning, having an extra blanket, sweater or other warm covering with you can make the difference between a pleasant outing and an unpleasant one.

A WEATHER SHIELD. If it's windy, raining or snowing hard, be sure you pack the weather shield (a special plastic covering with airholes, designed to fit over the pushchair).

A DUMMY, if the baby uses one. And an extra one in case she drops it.

ENTERTAINMENT. In the pushchair, a baby is usually content just to watch the world roll by. But in the car, it makes sense to bring along lightweight toys for him to swat or poke at. Also bring along rattles, stuffed animals or other small toys for him to shake or mouth when you get where you're going.

BABY-SAFE SUNSCREEN. Use a small amount of sunscreen on the baby's face, hands and other exposed skin year-round, whenever the sun is out.

OTHER TOILETRIES AND FIRST-AID ITEMS. You never know when you're going to need them, so it's smart to pack nappy rash ointment or cream, bandages and antibiotic ointment (especially once the baby has started crawling). Don't forget to bring along any medication the baby is taking if you'll be out when the next dose is due (if it needs to stay cool, put it in an insulated container with an ice pack).

TOO MANY CHORES

Q '*The parents give me so many errands to run and so much housework to do that I don't have much quality time to spend with the baby. Should I say something to the parents, or just do the best I can the way things are?*'

A It's hard being a working parent (as you well know if you have children of your own). Between the demands of business and baby, it's sometimes impossible to find time for life's other responsibilities – like picking up prescriptions, buying groceries and keeping on top of the laundry. That's why many working parents depend on their childcare provider to do a whole lot more than provide childcare.

How much is too much to ask? While asking you to do housework or errands that directly involve the child in your care (like keeping the baby's room clean or running to the store to pick up formula) is probably fair, asking you to run the whole household probably isn't. Too heavy a workload can also, as you say, cut into your quality time with baby.

So, if you're being asked to do more non-childcare tasks than you signed up for, speak to the parents. Chances are, they'd rather you spend more time with their child and less time running errands.

Do remember, though, that you can still interact with the baby while you're on the run. Point out the sights and sounds of the supermarket to the baby, sing songs while you're walking to the pharmacy or give a blow-by-blow while you fold laundry or wash dishes.

on the move

SAFE AND SOUND

Whenever you take the baby out for a stroll or a ride in the car, remember these all-important safety tips.

IN A PUSHCHAIR:

■ Always buckle the baby into the pushchair.

■ Never move the pushchair without making sure the baby is securely seated and buckled. The tiniest bump on the pavement could throw her out of the seat without warning.

■ Never place a newborn (under three months old) in a pushchair that doesn't recline.

■ Never store items (such as a nappy bag, stuffed animals or extra blankets) inside the pram with the baby. If they move onto the baby's face when you're not looking they could cause suffocation. Most prams and pushchairs have storage compartments under the seat or along the handle.

■ To make sure that the pushchair doesn't tip over, don't hang anything heavy on the handles or overstuff the net storage bag.

■ Keep your eyes and a hand on the pushchair at all times – even when you're sitting on a park bench or checking out some clothes in a shopping mall. A pram or pushchair can too easily be rolled away by someone other than you. Leaving a baby alone – even just for a quick moment – could lead to tragedy.

■ Use the pushchair wheel brakes when you need them (when you've stopped on a hill, for instance, or 'parked' the pushchair in the playground).

■ Make sure a foldable pushchair is fully locked or correctly snapped into the open position before putting the baby in it.

■ When folding or unfolding the pushchair, be sure the baby's hands are far away from areas that could pinch tiny fingers.

IN A CARRIER:

- Always bend at the knees (not at the waist) to pick something up so the baby doesn't slide out of the carrier.

- Stay off stools and ladders when using a baby carrier.

- Never use a baby carrier instead of a car seat.

- Never run with the baby in a carrier.

- Never carry a hot drink while you're toting the baby in a carrier.

- Don't keep the baby in a carrier or sling (particularly one made of a heavy fabric like corduroy) for long periods on warm days. Check often for signs of overheating (see page 98).

- Be sure the baby's head and shoulders are well supported in the carrier.

IN A CAR SEAT:

- Ask the parents to show you how to install the car seat and strap in the baby before you go out with him on your own.

- Never put a baby or child in the front seat of a car. Place the car seat, if at all possible, in the middle of the backseat.

- Always strap the baby into the car seat, even if you're just driving a block away or driving slowly (most accidents occur within 25 miles of the home and at slow speeds), even if the baby is crying.

- Adjust the shoulder harness on the car seat to fit the baby. The harness slots should be at or below the baby's shoulders; the harness buckle should be at hip level, not resting over the tummy; and the straps should be tightened so you can't get more than two fingers between the harness and the baby's collarbone.

- Dress the baby in clothes that allow straps to go between her legs. In cold weather, place blankets on top of the strapped-in baby (after adjusting the harness straps snugly).

- For a very young baby, use the special cushioned inserts so her head doesn't flop over.

- Never attach a car seat to a shopping cart, because the weight of the car seat can cause the cart to tip over – baby and all.

6 to 12 months

An outing with a newborn means getting some fresh air. An outing with an older baby means going on an expedition to an exciting new world.

DON'T LEAVE HOME WITHOUT ...

If you thought an infant's nappy bag was jam-packed, just wait until you stock the bag these days – with all those items you've got used to lugging along (see pages 99–101 if you need a reminder) plus more:

A MEAL. With the baby on solids, a bottle may not be enough when you're out and about. You may also have to plan on where that next meal is going to come from.

out and about

SAFE AND SOUND

Leave the child-proofed home, and the opportunities for trouble multiply. Remember the important safety tips outlined on pages 102–103 as well as the following when taking an older baby out and about:

■ Never leave the baby alone outside – even for just a moment, and even if she's sleeping.

■ Keep the baby within reach – and eyeshot – at all times. Not only can he get tangled in the harness or climb out of a parked pushchair, but it takes only a second for someone to snatch him away. Never turn your back or eyes away from the baby, even for a moment. Not in the playground, at the shopping mall or in the garden.

■ Find a baby-friendly playground. Choose one that has a separate area for small children (so the big kids on roller-blades and skateboards can't knock them over),

Be sure to pack a jar of baby food (an unopened jar doesn't need refrigeration, though you'll need to bin any leftovers) or a container of whatever the baby's on-the-go meal will be. Don't forget to use an ice pack and thermal bag to keep prepared food fresh.

SNACKS. Between meals, babies who have moved to finger foods always welcome a handy snack. Bring along some rice cakes, Cheerios or wholesome crackers.

A SPOON. That jar of baby food won't get you very far without something to feed it with. You can toss the dirty spoon in one of those small plastic bags until you get home to wash it.

A BOTTLE OR CUP for formula, breast milk, juice or water.

A BIB. Pack the disposable kinds or a regular one from home.

PAPER TOWELS (or extra wipes) for clean-up .

---

that is clean and well maintained, and that meets essential safety standards for swings, slides and other play equipment.

■ Before you cross the street, tell the baby you're waiting for the red light to change to green. And even if there are no walk lights, tell her you're looking both ways before you cross.

■ Watch out for nibbles. Most babies think a bite or two of anything is worth a try, even if it comes from a bush. Again and again, they have to be reminded that it's not okay to eat any plants, indoors or out. And never let baby crawl around shrubbery (or, for that matter, anywhere) without constant supervision.

■ Check public play areas before you let the baby go crawling. There might be dangers underfoot: dog droppings, old cigarette butts and broken glass that can hurt a baby's tender skin — or worse, go into a baby's mouth.

■ Reinforce playground safety rules by telling the baby not to walk in front of a moving swing and not to wait at the bottom of the slide.

1 to 3 years

Get ready. An outing with a toddler often means he'll want to be on his own two feet – which means you'll have to be on your toes, ready to run after him when he rushes to the swings, makes a dash for the nearest dog or lunges at the chocolate display in the checkout aisle.

WHAT THE TODDLER SHOULD WEAR

Toddlers (and those who care for them) need to get out of the house every day, even when it's hot or cold. To make sure toddlers can weather that fresh air, no matter what the temperature, dress properly for outings.

IN COLD WEATHER. When taking a toddler out in cold weather, don't forget:

- *A hat.* Because much of the body's heat is lost through the head, toddlers should wear hats at all times in the winter and even on chilly fall days.

- *Layers.* Multiple layers help to trap warm air. Putting the toddler in a vest, a top, a sweater and a jacket will keep him much warmer than just a top and a heavy jacket.

winning the mitten wars

TRICKS OF THE TRADE

Toddlers rarely like getting dressed – especially in bulky clothing. Next time you're waging war with a snowsuit or a pair of mittens or boots, try launching a silliness campaign instead. Put the coat on your head, the mittens on your ears, the boots on the doll's feet. Get those giggles going – and the toddler may just forget to put up a fight.

driving smart

Always follow these safety rules when taking a child in a car:

SAFE AND SOUND

■ Be sure the child is properly buckled into a car seat or booster in the backseat of the car.

  ■ You and other adult passengers should always wear seat belts (not only because it's the law, but also because in an accident, adults without belts can be thrown into – and hurt – a properly seated child).

■ A child should never be left alone in a car, not even for a moment.

■ Put any heavy objects in the boot or make sure they're secured. If you stop short or crash, heavy luggage or even a can from a shopping bag can go flying through the air.

■ Keep your eyes on the road and your hands on the wheel. If a child needs your attention, pull over to a safe spot on the roadside.

■ *Mittens.* She won't like to wear them, but she won't last long outside without them.

■ *Socks and boots.* Keeping a toddler's toes warm will keep the rest of his body warm. Make sure boots are waterproof; if they're not, come back inside as soon as the socks get wet.

IN HOT WEATHER. When taking a toddler out in hot weather, don't forget to:

■ Keep it light. There's no reason he should wear more than you would on a warm day.

■ Use sunscreen. Always.

■ Put on those shades. A toddler's eyes are sensitive, so it's a good idea to bring along a pair of toddler-sized sunglasses for sunshiny days. (If you wear shades, too, the toddler's more likely to cooperate with you.)

PAYBACK TIME

Q *'There are days when the parents don't leave me enough money to cover all the errands they ask me to do, so I end up using some of my own. I don't mind, but sometimes they forget to pay me back.'*

A After a long day at work and a commute home, it's easy for parents to forget to pay you back. To make it easier for them to remember, save all the receipts (from the supermarket, the pizza store, the ice-cream van). Submit your expenses in writing each day or at the end of the week, with a friendly reminder of how much they owe you. You may also want to ask the parents to give you more spending money at the beginning of the week so you don't have to dip into your own pocket. Whichever system you use, keep track of what you spend.

4 to 6 years

Too big for pushchairs, too big to be carried (though they may still want to be sometimes), this age group is easier than toddlers to take on outings. And more fun, too, since they're more cooperative and better behaved (mostly).

DON'T LEAVE HOME WITHOUT . . .

Gone are the days of the nappy bag, but you still can't leave the house empty-handed. Whenever you're out and about with a young child, you should pack:

- A picnic lunch (if your outing takes you out at midday)

- A few healthy snacks

- A drink of water or a juice box

- A change of clothes (if the child is still having accidents or if an activity might leave him wet or extremely dirty)

- Sunscreen

- Insect repellent, if needed

- Entertainment, such as a travel game or toy (if there's a chance the child might get bored)

FIELD TRIP FUN

Even a routine outing can be a field trip. A trip to the supermarket, for example, is an opportunity to teach a child about different foods and their colours, smells and textures. It's also a maths lesson (when you count out 5 apples or 8 carrots, when you give the clerk a £20 note and get back £15 change).

But don't stop at everyday outings. With the parents' okay, schedule occasional field trips that take the child to places that are new or exciting. Here are some ideas:

■ Petting zoo

■ Science museum

■ Bakery

■ Art museum

■ Planetarium

■ Art galleries

■ Library

■ Aquarium

■ Fire station

■ Farmer's market

■ Local sporting events

■ Children's museum

■ Any neighbourhood place that offers tours for children

STRANGER SMARTS

Q *'The parents and I have discussed ways to teach their children about the dangers of talking to or going with strangers. But I'm not sure how to warn the children without scaring them.'*

A When it comes to strangers, your job is to teach caution, not fear. Telling scary stories about strangers hurting children or taking them away can create unnecessary anxiety. While it's important for children to know that there are some people who are not nice and who might try to hurt them, it's just as important to let them know that most adults are good people who love kids. So teach the rules on pages 110–111, but don't go overboard with warnings. Too much fear will keep young children up at night – and keep them from feeling safe outside of their homes. Children this age think (as they should) that the world is a happy and safe place. In an effort to keep them safe, it's important not to rob them of that joy.

WHAT EVERY CHILD SHOULD KNOW ABOUT GETTING LOST

Because it takes only a second for an active, curious child to wander off on his own, make sure he knows what to do if he becomes lost. Compare notes with the parents and reinforce what they have already taught their child.

STAY PUT. Teach the child never to leave the shop, playground or park if she becomes separated from you. Remind her that you'll be looking for her.

CALL FOR ME. Tell the child to call out your name, loudly.

FIND A 'MUMMY' FIGURE. Teach him to tell a 'mommy-like' person with children that he's lost.

stranger danger

SAFE AND SOUND

There's more to keeping a young child safe when out and about than just watching him swing from the monkey bars or climb up the slide (though you should always be watching that). Ensuring that he doesn't get lost or, even worse, get snatched by someone else is your highest priority – on a bustling city street or in a quiet suburban park.

Keep an eye on the child at all times while reinforcing these basic safety rules:

■ **DON'T TALK TO STRANGERS.** Remind the child never to talk to strangers unless she's right next to a grown-up she knows. Let her know that a stranger is *any* person she doesn't know – not just the scary bogeyman she imagines a stranger to be.

■ **DON'T ACCEPT ANYTHING FROM A STRANGER.** Teach the child to run away from any person he doesn't know who wants to give him something – even if it's a tempting present or sweets. Let the child know it's okay to scream for help if the stranger insists. But also let him know it's okay to accept something from another person if you say it's allowed.

FIND A PERSON IN CHARGE. If the child cannot find a 'mummy', teach him to go to a uniformed security guard, a police officer or a salesperson with a name tag.

LOOKING FOR A LOST CHILD

If you can't find a child in a crowded place, you'll need to know exactly what to do.

STAY CALM. Take a deep breath, then concentrate on looking for the child.

CALL OUT. Even if the child can't see you, she might be able to hear you. Call out her name in a calm but loud voice.

SEEK HELP. There's only so much territory you can cover yourself. So notify the security guard at the

- **NEVER GO ANYWHERE WITH A STRANGER.** Remind the child that she should never get into someone's car unless you say it's okay. Tell her never to help a stranger (with directions, or to find a lost dog) unless you're with her.

- **STAY CLOSE BY.** Before each outing, remind the child that he needs to stay close to you, and explain that this is so he doesn't get lost. It will be easier for you to keep him near if you make sure he stays busy during your outings.

- **KEEP AN EYE ON ME.** Teach the child that she should always be able to see you and be heard by

you. If the swings are on the other side of the playground, don't let the child go there unless she can see you clearly (and call for you) from that distance. It goes without saying that the same holds true for you.

- **DON'T BE AFRAID TO 'TELL'.** This is one case when 'telling' is always a good idea. Let the child know that he should always tell you when something happens that doesn't 'feel right' or makes him at all uncomfortable.

Remember, even if the child has been taught all these safety rules, it is still *your* responsibility to keep a child safe from all dangers, including strangers.

on the go with young children

Young children like to be independent – but that doesn't mean they can be on their own when you're out and about. To play it safe:

■ Follow all of the parents' safety rules.

■ Always hold a child's hand when crossing a street. Be sure to teach them pedestrian safety (look both ways before crossing, listen for a car coming, wait for the green man), but don't count on her to always remember the rules.

SAFE AND SOUND

■ Make sure the child always wears a bicycle helmet when riding a bike.

■ Avoid cycling near traffic.

■ When out roller-skating or roller-blading (or if scooters are permitted), make sure the child uses the proper safety equipment, including a helmet, kneepads and elbow pads.

■ Teach stranger awareness.

■ Teach water safety. Do not let the child play around any water (lake, pool, ocean and so on) without adult supervision (even if he's a good swimmer).

■ Closely supervise the child around unfamiliar dogs.

shopping mall, the lifeguard at the pool, a salesperson in the shop, or parents or care providers in the park that you've lost a child. Enlist as many people as you can to help look. (Remember to give a description of the child and details of what she's wearing.)

RETRACE YOUR STEPS. Where did you last see the child? Go back there to search. Or look in a place where you think the child might be. If he loves the swings at the playground, go there. If she's into Barbie dolls, check out that section of the store.

CALL THE POLICE. If the child isn't found within a few minutes, call 999.

PUBLIC BATHROOMS

Q *'When I'm in a public place with the six-year-old boy I look after and he needs to use the toilet, I feel uneasy about letting him go to the men's room alone. I try to get him to go before we leave home, but this rarely works. What can I do?'*

A You're right to be wary. An adult should always accompany a child to a public lavatory (unless it's an individual, self-contained toilet such as those found at petrol stations). Of course, as you've noticed, the tricky part is convincing an easily embarrassed young boy that he's better off in the ladies' room with you than in the men's room without you.

One way to avoid such a problem is to choose child-friendly destinations that have 'family' toilets – individual toilets for children and their parents or care provider to use. If that's not in the cards, wait until the ladies' toilet is empty and take the child in with you. Explain to him that the ladies' toilet has individual stalls for privacy. If he insists on going to the men's room (clear this with the parents first), wait until the toilet is completely empty, then stand by the opened door. Ask any man who wants to use the toilet to wait until the child is finished.

the safety police

TRICKS OF THE TRADE

Young children love to be in charge – and to be big helpers. To make them more cooperative when it comes to car safety, appoint them to the Safety Police in charge of making sure that everyone (including you) is buckled up and that the doors are locked before the car starts moving. You can use this trick when walking, too. Before crossing streets, the Safety Police can watch for 'the green man' or remind you to 'stop, listen and look both ways.'

bathing

for some children, it's a wet wonderland from start to finish. For others, taking the plunge is the scary part; once they're in the tub, they're happy as clams. For still others (and their care providers), cleaning up their acts is a dreaded ordeal. Still, as long as children get dirty (and they always will), they need to be bathed. Here's all you need to know to make bathtime a fun and safe time for you and the children you're sudsing up.

newborn to 6 months

Are you on bath duty? Here's a quick how-to on bathing the littlest babies.

PICK THE RIGHT TIME. Giving a bath just before bedtime (or a nap) will help the baby to relax and sleep better.

PICK THE RIGHT LOCATION. Newborn babies can take a bath in the kitchen or bathroom sink or in a baby bath. When an older baby moves to a regular bathtub, place a mat or folded towel under his bottom so he doesn't slip. Once he can sit without help, a bath seat that attaches to the bottom of the tub will keep him upright (but remember – you must keep one hand on him at all times).

WARM THE AIR. For the baby's comfort, especially in the early months, keep the room where you're doing the bathing warm (75° to 80°F, if possible) and draught-free.

BE PREPARED. Have all of the following ready *before* undressing the baby:

■ Baby soap and shampoo

■ Two washcloths (one will do if you use your hand for soaping)

■ Cotton balls for cleaning the eyes

■ Towel, preferably with a hood

■ Clean nappy and clothing

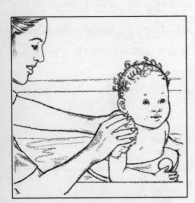

Even if the baby is strapped into a bath seat, never take your eyes off her during bathtime. She can slip out of the bath seat and drown in just a few inches of water.

NOT TOO DEEP. Run enough water into the baby tub so that half of baby's body will be underwater. Before you add the baby, check the water with your elbow; it should be warm but not hot. A baby's skin is much more easily burned than an adult's.

GIVE SUPPORT. Place the baby slowly into the bath, talk calmly to reassure her, and hold on tight so she doesn't startle and jump out of your hands. Support her neck and head with one hand unless the tub has built-in support (see below).

WASH UP. Start with the cleanest areas (eyes, face and ears), then move on to the arms, neck, legs, back and abdomen, and finally clean the dirtiest areas (penis or vagina and buttocks). Though you won't need to use soap every day on most of the body (except for allover 'accidents'), be sure to use it on hands and the nappy area daily.

did you know?

Until a baby starts crawling and getting dirty, a daily bath isn't needed. Spot cleaning during nappy changes and after feedings – with a bath a few times a week – will keep her looking and smelling fresh.

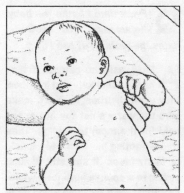

Offer support when placing the baby in the bathtub and throughout the bath.

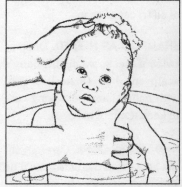

Until the baby can control his head, hold it steady with one hand while washing him.

suds sense

Getting wet is fun, but safety must come first when you combine water, soap and a tiny baby. Keep these tips in mind:

■ Give the baby's bathtime all your attention. Don't be hurried.

■ Never leave the baby unattended in the bath *even for a second* to take care of something else. Don't answer the phone, and don't take your hands off the baby for any reason – even to reach for a towel (have it nearby before you start the bath). That goes, too, for a baby who's sitting in a bath seat.

■ Never run the water with the baby in the bath. You never know when the temperature might change.

■ Don't add baby soap or bubble bath to the water – it can dry the baby's delicate skin.

SAFE AND SOUND

RINSE AWAY. Use a fresh wash-cloth to rinse the baby thoroughly of all traces of soap.

SHAMPOO AS NEEDED. Once or twice a week, wash the baby's scalp and hair (if he has any) with baby shampoo, taking care to keep it out of his eyes.

AND YOU'RE DONE. Carefully lift the baby from the bath (she'll be slippery), dry her off, put on her nappy and clothes.

BATHTIME BLUES

Q *'Every time I bathe the baby, she screams. I just know she hates the bath. What can I do?'*

A First, ask the parents if they have better luck – and if so, how they work their magic. Next, make sure the water's not too hot or too cold (or the room too chilly). Then try distracting her with a toy, music or funny faces. If she still fusses, switch to a sponge bath for a while. Eventually, with patience – and more toys – bathtime will become fun time.

6 to 12 months

Once the baby can sit, bath-time is no longer a chore for either of you – it's a time to splash, sail and have a blast. Here are some suggestions for making rub-a-dub-dubbing fun for every-one involved.

THROW IN THE TOYS. Bath toys (rubber duckies, sponges, squirt-ing animals, and so on) provide endless entertainment. But if you don't have any of those on hand, plastic cups and containers can get the giggles going just as fast. And while the baby is busy with all the toys, you'll have time to get in a good scrub (which will probably be needed if he's been crawling on those knees all day).

MAKE A SPLASH. Let the baby splash around – even if it means you get wet – but don't splash back just yet. Chances are he'll be con-fused by that – or even frightened.

DON'T PUT BABY OUT WITH THE BATHWATER. Wait until the baby's out of the bath before you open the drain. The rush of the water and the noise may be scary.

don't sweat getting wet

Want to know how to keep bathtime safe and fun for both you and the baby? Try these tricks:

TRICKS OF THE TRADE

■ Keep bath toys clean (so germs don't grow) by letting them dry in a net or basket after the bath. Toys that trap water need to be cleaned regularly with a solution of 1 part bleach to 15 parts water, then rinsed well.

■ Wear a plastic apron if the baby loves to splash in the bath. Or keep a spare outfit to change into in case you get wet.

1 to 3 years

Many toddlers have a love–hate relationship with the bath. They hate the idea of getting into the bath, but once they're in, they love it so much there's no getting them out. So while the toddler's turning into a prune, try these bathtime activities:

■ Demonstrate how some objects sink (the sort of plastic ring you would toss into a pool) while other objects (an empty, capped shampoo bottle) float.

■ Show the child what happens when you turn over a cup filled with water – and learn about cause and effect.

■ Blow soap bubbles and watch them soar through the air above the bathtub, then land in the water and float. Popping them will make the game even more fun!

■ Let clean sponges get filled with water, then let the toddler squeeze them out – and then start all over again!

■ Use special coloured soap and watch as the water turns from clear to coloured. Coloured soap can also be used to decorate the bath.

■ Show the toddler how to rub soapy hands together to make suds.

Tots and the Tub

SAFE AND SOUND

To make sure bathtime is as safe as it is fun:

■ Never turn your back on a toddler who's in the bath, even for a moment.

■ Never leave the bathroom when a toddler is in the bath – even just to grab a towel or answer the phone. A three-year-old can drown in a few inches of water.

4 to 6 years

Will it be a bath or a shower? Some young children still love long soaks (and splashes) in the bath, while others prefer the quicker in-and-out of a shower. A lot depends on whether or not the child can wash by himself.

As a general rule, most four-year-olds will still be taking baths and will need help soaping up, shampooing and rinsing. Five-year-olds may be capable of washing themselves, but you'll still need to be in the bathroom and help out from time to time – especially when a shampoo is on the agenda. Many six-year-olds enjoy showering by themselves, while others (especially boys) resist bathing altogether and will often have to be reminded to wash every part of their body.

PRIVACY, PLEASE

Q *'I childmind a six-year-old boy, and his parents want me to see that he has a shower every night. Doesn't he need his privacy at this age?'*

A Many six-year-olds insist on privacy when they shower – and that means you're outta there. But for safety's sake, and in case he needs help, you still have to stand by the slightly open bathroom door. Remind him as he showers to rinse all the shampoo out of his hair, and to wash his bottom and give his knees a good scrub.

- Never let a toddler play in the bathroom or go near the bath (empty or full) without you.

- Don't use a hairdryer or other electrical equipment near the bath or water. Make sure all appliances near the bath are unplugged.

- Clear the bath area of any dangerous items, such as razors, scissors or clippers.

- Make sure the bathroom door can't be locked from the inside or that you know how to unlock it from the outside.

sleeping

there are good sleepers, and not-so-good sleepers. Children who conk out the moment their tiny heads hit the mattress, and others who battle the sandman even when they're too exhausted to keep their little eyes open. Those who take to bed happily, and those who put up a struggle every inch of the way (one more story! one more drink of water! one more lullaby!). No matter what kind of sleeper you have on your hands, you can help make naptime and bedtime a dream.

newborn to 6 months

Newborns often seem to sleep the day away, waking only to be fed and changed (and of course to cry). But as they get older, a pattern of sleep and awake time begins to develop and your day becomes somewhat more predictable – and a lot more fun.

NAPTIME. Though there's little rhyme or reason to the nap

off to dreamland

Naptime or bedtime, here's how to make sure the baby sleeps safely:

- **BACK TO SLEEP.** Always put the baby on his back to sleep. Babies who sleep on their stomach are at risk of SIDS (sudden infant death syndrome).

- **SWADDLE SNUGLY (AND SAFELY).** Some babies will be happier on their back (and sleep better) if they're swaddled. But stop swaddling once the baby is active enough to kick off the covers (loose blankets can be dangerous in a crib).

SAFE AND SOUND

- **BACK TO SLEEP FOR FLIPPERS, TOO.** Even after the baby has started rolling over, continue to put her down on her back – and let her decide about flipping.

- **KEEP BEDDING OUT OF THE COT.** Never place the baby in a cot with pillows, comforters, fluffy blankets or stuffed animals, because of the risk of suffocation. If it's cool in the room, just dress him in a warm Babygro. Also, make sure the bumpers are tied tightly (or snapped on) to the cot's sides.

- **STAY NEARBY.** You should be close enough at all times to hear the baby's cries before they turn into ear-piercing wails; if there's an intercom, keep it turned on and close by.

schedule of a baby under three months, you'll see some regularity by the time she gets closer to four months. For many babies it goes something like this: awake two hours, asleep two hours. (This pattern varies widely depending on the baby and on the parents' ideas about sleep. Generally, it's best to follow the baby's cues.)

It's not a good idea to keep the baby awake during the day so she can sleep better at night. An overtired baby has a harder time falling asleep and staying asleep. On the other hand, a well-rested baby actually sleeps longer and better. Too much napping, however, can keep baby and her parents up at night – especially if it's too close to bedtime.

BEDTIME. Sleeping habits among infants vary widely. Some are sleeping through the night; many aren't. Some have been started on a bedtime routine – a bath, a bottle, a lullaby and then down to sleep, for instance. Others might expect to be rocked to sleep.

BACK TO SLEEP

Q *'I haven't taken care of a baby for quite a while, so I was surprised to hear that babies are now supposed to be put on their back to sleep. I always put my baby on her tummy – and she slept much better than the baby I care for now.'*

A Things change quickly in the baby business – and one of the biggest changes in recent times has been the recommendation that babies always be

did you know?

Do you ever get the feeling that babies are always sleeping – yet never for very long? Even though most newborns sleep 16 to 18 hours a day, they tend to take those rests two to three hours at a time. Gradually, they begin to sleep less, but for longer stretches. By three months, they need about 15 hours of sleep – approximately 9 hours at night plus three 2-hour daytime naps. And by six months, most babies are sleeping for even longer stretches at night and getting through the day on just two naps of 2 hours each.

keeping a good baby down

TRICKS OF THE TRADE

Does this sound familiar? You spend 15 minutes rocking the baby in aching arms until she finally falls asleep. Ready to make the break and give your arms a rest, you lay her ever so carefully in her cot – but the minute her head touches the mattress, her eyes pop open. She's wide awake – and probably crying. The problem? She was still in light sleep mode when you let her go. The solution? Make sure the baby is in a deep sleep before laying her down. A sure-fire way to be certain she's really off to dreamland is to gently lift her arm or leg. If it feels limp and flops back down – and she doesn't jerk it – she's out. Now's the time to lay her down to sleep.

placed on their back to sleep. This position greatly reduces the risk of SIDS (sudden infant death syndrome). But make sure the baby in your care spends supervised time on his tummy while he's awake. The motto now? 'Back to sleep, tummy to play.'

SLEEP SCHEDULES

Q *'I'm childminding a three-month-old who doesn't have any real sleep schedule. Shouldn't there be one by now? I always thought that babies without schedules ended up spoiled.'*

A The best schedule for a baby that young is the one he sets for himself (no matter how irregular and unreliable it is). At this point, he still needs to be fed when he's hungry and to sleep when he's sleepy. In a month or two, you'll start to see a more regular pattern of eating and sleeping emerge. In the meantime, try to keep him from catnapping (in the carriage on the way to the market, for instance), since many short naps can interfere with good, long sleeps. (That's easier said than done, so see the tips on page 129 for keeping the baby from kitten-napping.)

6 to 12 months

Some babies are big sleepers; others seem to get by on very little. How a baby sleeps during the day can affect how she'll sleep at night (which affects how her parents sleep, which will definitely affect their mood each morning). Be sure to ask the parents how they want sleep handled on your watch (when and how long the baby should nap during the day, what time she should be put down to sleep at night and what to do if she resists going to sleep). Here's the general scoop on how babies sleep during the second six months:

NAPTIME. Most babies will continue to take two daytime naps through their first birthday, though how long those naps last will vary widely from child to child. If the baby is taking both a morning and afternoon nap, begin the afternoon nap before

snug as a bug

SAFE AND SOUND

Now that the baby can pull up, the cot becomes more than just a place to sleep. It's also a place to play in – and try to climb out of. Here's how to keep baby safe:

■ Check the mattress supports to be sure they're not loose.

■ Take out escape routes. Big toys or fluffy pillows or comforters don't belong in the cot. Not only are they unsafe, but babies can use them as ladders to freedom over the side.

■ Protect the very active climber by putting pillows or cushions on the floor to break the fall in case the baby does make a successful escape. Also make sure the mattress is set at the lowest level.

3 P.M. (unless you've been told otherwise) or she'll resist sleep at night.

BEDTIME. By nine months, most babies sleep a total of 14 hours a day. And the goal is to get in as many of those hours as possible at night – preferably all of them in a row. In general, night wakings will gradually decrease as the baby gives up night feedings. Some babies continue to take night feedings throughout the second half of the first year (although, unless they were premature, they probably do it more out of habit than need). By age one, a baby usually sleeps a little over 13½ hours a day, with (hopefully) 11 of those hours at night. A bedtime ritual becomes more important than ever and helps to ensure a better night's sleep for all.

SLEEP TRAINING

Q *'The parents have decided to sleep-train their baby and have told me to let her cry herself to sleep. But it's so hard for me to listen to her cry.'*

A Rest assured, baby's crying is tougher on you than it is on her. And it won't last long. As soon as she learns how to fall asleep on her own, without being picked up, rocked or otherwise comforted, the crying will stop – probably within a couple of weeks and maybe much sooner. In the meantime, try lowering the volume on the intercom slightly, using earplugs or turning on the TV or radio. (The idea is to take the edge off the sound, not to block it entirely.) If you notice a change in the cry – it becomes more high-pitched, more frantic – do a quick check to make sure the baby hasn't got into trouble (pulled herself up and can't get back down, for instance). Also, ask the parents what strategies they use for coping with crying and how long they expect the sleep training to take.

KITTEN-NAPPING

Q *'The parents don't want their daughter napping on the go. But she often falls asleep in the pushchair on the way home from the park – even when it's not her regular naptime.'*

A Sounds like you have a kitten-napper on your hands. See if the parents have a good solution. If not, try keeping her awake by bringing along some toys, singing some lively songs or pointing out sights and sounds on your excursions. If that doesn't work, let her fall asleep in the pushchair and then wake her when you return home. Put her down for her next nap a little earlier to get her back on schedule. (Do run this plan by the parents first, though.)

Keep in mind that the best way to avoid kitten-napping is to take your park outing immediately *after* a nap so baby will be less likely to fall asleep.

CRIB COMFORT

Q *'Every time I put the baby to sleep in his cot, I can't help but worry that's he's uncomfortable without a pillow and blanket.'*

A He's not uncomfortable, and since he's slept flat and uncovered on the mattress since birth, he doesn't know any better. More important, placing a pillow or blanket in the crib with a young baby increases the risk of suffocation and SIDS (sudden infant death syndrome). When he's older, you can let him cosy up to a pillow and blanket. But for now, keep them out of the cot.

1 to 3 years

Toddlers still need plenty of sleep to keep those motors running – 10 to 12 hours at night, plus at least 1 to 2 hours of daytime sleep. But by around 18 months, most toddlers typically give up one of their naps, and by age three or four, they often stop napping altogether (it was nice while it lasted).

NAPTIME. A slowdown in naps is normal during the second and third years, since toddlers need less daytime sleep. Of course, they almost always need more than they'd like, and they often resist going down for a nap (so much to do, and you want me to lie down in a dark room?). To counter that resistance, try helping a toddler unwind before naptime with quiet music, quiet stories, quiet activities.

BEDTIME. Since toddlers would always rather be on the go than stop for sleep, very few actually look forward to bedtime – and many will fight sleep with their last ounce of strength, no matter how exhausted they are. For best results, stick to a relaxing routine that slows down that perpetual-motion machine before trying to put her to bed.

A CRANKY TODDLER

Q *'The parents have asked me not to let their three-year-old nap during the day because they want him to sleep better at night. I completely understand, but I'm at my wit's end trying to entertain him when he gets cranky in the afternoon.'*

A When one nap is too many but no nap leaves the child cranky, it's time to replace naptime with quiet time. Quiet time can give him a chance to recharge without sleep – and hopefully keep the crankies at bay. Before he begins to unravel, help him unwind with 45 minutes of peaceful activities. Curl up on the couch for some stories, or do some

a big move

Switching from a cot to a bed is a big move for a little toddler, and it's usually made sometime during the second or third year, depending on when the child is ready. While some toddlers embrace their new digs and are proud of graduating to a 'big boy (or girl)' bed, others find it hard to cosy up to the new, wide-open spaces. You can help the parents and child make the transition from cot to bed easier:

TRICKS OF THE TRADE

■ **SOUND THE ALARM.** Let the parents know if the child is climbing out (or trying to climb out) of his cot at naptime. If he is, it's probably time for the move to a big bed. If he's content to stay put and doesn't seem to have outgrown the cot, there's no rush to push him out, even if the toddler next door has already traded up.

■ **MAKE FRIENDS WITH THE BED.** Have her help make the bed with you each morning (she can pick out favourite stuffed animals to 'keep it warm' until she returns at night). Encourage playing in her bed (tucking dollies in, playing house there), read her stories in bed before naptime, but never send her to bed as a punishment. It should be a happy place for her.

■ **PLAY UP THE POSITIVES.** Toddlers love being 'big'. So make a 'big' deal about graduating to a 'big boy (or girl)' bed.

■ **KEEP IT THE SAME.** Transitions are always easier when some things stay the same. For a smoother switch, keep regular nap or bedtime routines unchanged. And don't forget that special teddy or blanket.

colouring together. Even quiet playing (with puzzles or finger puppets) should keep him entertained without revving him up. You might also discuss with the parents the possibility of an earlier dinnertime and bedtime until the transition is complete.

4 to 6 years

For most infant-school children, naptime is over forever (though some children may continue with a 'rest time' until age five). And bedtime, well, it's often a time for trouble: struggles to get the child into bed; more struggles to keep him *in* bed. But if the parents agree, try making bedtime more peaceful by following this plan:

FOLLOW A ROUTINE. Prevent going-to-bed problems by sticking to a routine – perhaps a bath, toothbrushing, reading three books, talking about the day and turning out the light.

DON'T ALLOW 'JACK-IN-THE-BEDS'. Once the child is in bed, be strict about keeping him there. If he gets up and comes out, quickly return him to his room with a firm but calm voice: 'You may not leave your bed until morning (unless you have to use the bathroom).' Warn him that you'll have to close the door if he doesn't stay put.

HONOUR ONLY ONE REQUEST. Young children may come up with many excuses to avoid or prolong bedtime, including requests for glasses of water, to be 'tucked in' and so on. Do one special 'favour' and then no more.

IGNORE THE PROTESTS. If the child continues with the bedtime struggle, don't yell or plead. Stay calm, matter-of-fact, but firm. Keep your interactions with her to a minimum – no bedtime hug or kiss this time around. (Of course, you'll need to follow the parents' directions when it comes to bedtime struggles. Some parents might prefer that you sit quietly in the room or at the door until the child falls asleep.)

PRAISE. Remember to congratulate the child if he went to bed without protest the night before. A bedtime chart (with a sticker for each easy night of bedtime) may help to reinforce good bedtime habits.

NIGHTMARES

Nightmares are normal and common during the early school years when imaginations are active. To help a child have sweet dreams, you can:

KEEP THINGS CALM. Never bring fears up at bedtime, but if the child does, do some comforting. If she's worried about ghosts, reassure her that they're make-believe. If she's concerned about dogs, read a book about a girl and her friendly dog.

TRY PREVENTION. If the child is afraid of monsters, make sure he doesn't watch scary movies before bedtime. Also avoid fairy tales or games involving scary make-believe in the evening. Instead, tell the child you're giving him 'good dreams' with your kiss.

BANISH THE MONSTERS. Be creative and get rid of the monsters as part of the nighttime routine. Arm the child with a flashlight and a stuffed animal 'guard' to watch over her. Do a 'monster check' of the room, then offer a magic spray bottle (actually filled with water, maybe scented with lavender) to fight the monsters off. Making the child feel powerful may help her get over her fear.

LIGHTS ON. A night-light in the child's room (with the parents' go-ahead) can help him feel safer.

STAY CLOSE. Children often wake up from their nightmares upset and need some quiet reassurance. Stay nearby so the child doesn't wake up alone and afraid.

TALK ABOUT IT. Let the child talk about the nightmare before he goes back to sleep, or the next day. Remind him that all dreams are just make-believe stories – they're not real and they're not really happening.

OFFER COMFORT. Give the child a hug and reassure her that she's perfectly safe. Offer a glass of water or warm milk and another 'good dreams' kiss.

behaviour & discipline

Children will always keep you on your toes. One minute, a baby's smiling sweetly; next minute, he's wailing like a fire engine. One minute, a toddler's making crayon circles on a piece of paper; next minute, she's practising her drawing skills on the living room wall. One minute, a preschooler's playing teddy bear hospital; next minute, he's ripping the stethoscope off his playmate's neck. There's no predicting how a child will behave – but having a good idea of what to expect will help you cope with almost any kind of behaviour. So will arming yourself with effective discipline techniques.

newborn to 6 months

WHY IS BABY CRYING?

Crying is a newborn's way of talking. What's more, most babies have different cries to communicate different needs. If you're not sure, use this cheat sheet to crack the crying code:

THE 'I'M HUNGRY' CRY. A low-pitched cry that rises and falls rhythmically and has a pleading quality to it (as in 'Please, please feed me!') usually means the baby's in the market for a meal.

THE 'I'M IN PAIN' CRY. This cry – sudden, loud, panicked – leaves the baby breathless. The first long scream is followed by a pause and then long, high-pitched shrieks.

THE 'I'M BORED' CRY. This cry alternates between coos (as the newborn tries to get a good interaction going), fussing (when the attention he's craving isn't coming), loud crying ('Why are you ignoring me?') and whimpers ('C'mon, what's a baby got to do to get a cuddle around here?'). The boredom cry stops as soon as the baby is picked up.

THE 'I'M UNCOMFORTABLE OR OVERTIRED' CRY. This cry – whiny, nasal and continuous – usually builds in intensity. Time for a nap (or nappy change or toy swap).

THE 'I'M SICK' CRY. This cry is often weak, nasal-sounding and lower-pitched than the 'pain' or 'overtired' cry.

SOOTHING BABY'S CRY

As you get to know the baby in your care and learn one cry from another, you'll want to know just how to respond.

HUNGRY? If you think so, try a bottle. But don't always respond to tears with food. If you feed when the baby's not hungry, you'll end up overfeeding.

GASSY? Babies often cry when they're bothered by wind. Try to:

■ **Get a burp.** He may just need to release some air he swallowed while eating.

■ **Add some pressure** – to the baby's tummy, that is. If it's wind that's causing the crying, applying gentle pressure on her tummy might help to calm her. Try laying her, tummy down, across your lap. Or rub her tummy gently.

TIRED? An overtired baby may be too wound up to fall asleep. Try rocking him – in your arms, a pram, a cradle or a baby carrier – to calm him down before bedtime.

WET OR DIRTY? Some babies cry when their nappy is full.

TOO HOT OR TOO COLD? If the baby seems too warm (is she sweating? hot to the touch?), take off a layer or two of clothing, open the window or turn on a fan. If chilling is the problem (her neck or body feels cold to the touch), add a layer or turn up the heat.

BORED? In the early months, some infants are happy to sit and

never shake a baby

SAFE
AND
SOUND

Caring for a baby, especially one who does a lot of crying, can be very frustrating – even for the most patient care provider. But make sure you *never* take out your frustration on the baby by shaking him. Shaking a baby can cause brain damage or even death. If you're at your wit's end with a crying baby, calmly put him down in a safe spot (cot, strapped into an infant seat on the floor, playpen), walk out of the room, take a deep breath, count to 10, meditate for a minute – or do anything else to calm yourself down. If you can't calm the baby (or yourself), and especially if you have other children to care for, call the parents.

calming a crying baby

Here are some strategies to try when you're coping with crying:

■ **WALK THE FLOOR.** It's tried, tested and tiring -- back and forth you go, with the baby in a carrier or sling or in your arms.

■ **KEEP THE BABY IN MOTION.** Rhythmic rocking -- in your arms or in a pushchair, vibrating infant seat or baby swing (if he's old enough) -- often soothes.

■ **TAKE A TRIP.** Strap the baby into the car seat and drive around the neighbourhood until he calms down.

TRICKS OF THE TRADE

■ **PACIFY.** Babies often find comfort in sucking. Ask the parents if the baby can have a dummy or if you should help her find one of those tiny fingers to suck.

■ **WRAP HIM UP.** Swaddle the baby -- but only if the room is cool.

■ **GIVE A LITTLE CUDDLE.** Hold the baby pressed close to your chest with your arms wrapped around her.

■ **TRY A BATH.** A warm bath can work wonders.

■ **SING A SONG.** It could be a soft lullaby, a nursery rhyme or the latest chart topper.

■ **PUT ON THE VACUUM.** Or a fan, a clothes dryer, a tape of sounds from the uterus or from nature, a repeated whispered 'sh' or anything that has rhythm.

■ **MASSAGE AWAY.** Rub the baby's back, belly, arms and legs in a firm but gentle and loving way.

■ **RESORT TO RITUAL.** Some babies thrive on routine and are calmed by regular feeding, bathing, changing and outing times. If such routine works, stay with the programme -- some babies just need to know what to expect.

watch the world go by. Others need to be entertained and will cry out of frustration and boredom. You can try to stimulate a bored baby by:

- Carrying him around while describing what you're seeing and doing.

- Dancing gently with her to music. (Keep the volume low, since very loud music can damage baby's sensitive ears.)

- Playing with him (making funny faces, showing him toys, reciting silly rhymes).

- Changing her surroundings. If you've been in the house all day, head outside for a walk (weather permitting).

OVERSTIMULATED? What started out as fun (dancing, games, and so on) may have become too much for the baby to handle. An overstimulated baby may cry when he hits overload. Dim the lights and start bringing on the quiet comfort.

SPOILING BABY

Q *'The parents have told me to pick up their newborn every time he cries. That's fine with me – but I wonder if I'll be spoiling the baby.'*

A You can't spoil a young infant. Babies need to know that their calls will be answered. What's more, a quick response now will pay off later. Babies whose needs are met promptly are likely to grow into more secure, less demanding children.

did you know?

If a baby cries inconsolably for three hours or more a day, she may have colic. No one knows what causes colic (and why some babies have it, and others don't), but one thing is sure – it's nobody's fault. Colic simply happens. Here's the bad news: caring for a colicky baby isn't easy (though the tips on the opposite page will help). The good news: colic usually gets as bad as it's going to get by 3 weeks and starts to go away by 12 weeks. Most babies are colic-free, or almost, by the fourth month. So hang in there!

And here's a bonus: Babies whose cries are regularly answered will cry less as toddlers.

Keep in mind, too, that the longer you let a baby cry, the harder it is to figure out *why* he's crying.

Sometimes, once a baby has got all worked up, even he may forget what all the fuss was about. And a baby who's been left to cry may have a harder time calming down.

6 to 12 months

IT'S HARD TO SEPARATE

Does the baby cry every time Mummy or Daddy leaves the house? During the second six months, almost all babies experience separation anxiety. They've learned what it means when their parents leave – they remember them and miss them when they're gone. To help the baby (and the parents) have an easier time with those good-byes:

BE EARLY. Don't rush in just as the parents are rushing out. For the baby's sake, the handoff must be smooth and well planned. Hang out with the baby while the parents are still getting ready to go. Distract him with a shape sorter or a lively game of peekaboo. It'll be easier for him to say

good-bye if the two of you are having a great time playing.

BE LOVING. Keep the baby on your lap and give her lots of hugs. Be calm, warm and reassuring. Tell her about all the fun you'll have together.

BE HELPFUL. Talk for the baby: 'Mummy's coming home soon. Right, Mummy?' 'Daddy will be home at dinnertime.' 'I'm staying here to play games all day.'

BE PREDICTABLE. Create a good-bye ritual, such as blowing Mummy a kiss or saying, 'See you later, alligator.' In a few weeks, the baby may blow a kiss, too; in a few months, he may surprise you and say 'bye-bye' while watching and waving from the window.

what's scaring baby: a checklist

As babies get older and smarter, they grow more fearful – sometimes of things they liked in the past. Some babies are afraid of loud noises such as vacuuming; others are frightened by barking dogs. Still others start to cry when a sudden movement catches them off guard. Here's how you can help:

DO

☑ **DO UNDERSTAND.** A hug and an explanation will work wonders. Pick up the baby and explain what the noise was. But don't overdo the comfort – or the baby might think there really is something to be afraid of.

☑ **DO HELP.** You can help the baby get over her fear by letting her touch the vacuum when it's off. Have her wave to the dog – or even pet a very sweet one if she's feeling brave and you have the owner's permission. (Or pet the dog for her while you hold her safely in your arms.)

DON'T

☒ **DON'T TEASE.** It's not silly to be afraid of a big noisy vacuum or a loud barking dog when you're so little. Don't make fun of the baby's fear.

☒ **DON'T PUSH.** Forcing the baby to face her fears won't work – and could make things worse. If she's afraid of the vacuum, don't turn it on to help her get over her fear (use the machine while she naps). If it's the German shepherd next door that scares her, don't force her to pet it. Wait it out; in time she'll outgrow her fears.

DON'T TAKE IT PERSONALLY. Separation anxiety, which can continue throughout the first year and linger on through the toddler years, is a normal part of development. A baby who cries when his parents leave him with you isn't rejecting you – he's just rejecting the idea of being separated from his parents.

WHAT'S 'NO'?

Babies are too young for discipline. Though they may begin understanding the word 'no' before their first birthday, they certainly aren't ready to begin obeying it – or to follow rules of any kind. Nor do they understand the difference between right and wrong. A baby who turns his cup of juice over or reaches for a box on a supermarket shelf doesn't know any better – and shouldn't be expected to. Still, you can take advantage of these teachable moments by saying, 'Juice is for drinking, so it needs to stay in the cup,' or 'We need to leave those boxes on the shelf.' The seeds of discipline will come in handy when baby becomes a toddler.

1 to 3 years

If there's one thing that's predictable about toddlers, it's that they're unpredictable. They can go from whining and complaining to sweet and charming to kicking and screaming in 60 seconds flat – and 60 times in the space of a single morning. Yet, believe it or not, you can make sense of a toddler's behaviour.

MAKE 'NO' A 'YES'

In a toddler's normal fight for independence, the word 'no' is a favourite battle cry. Still, you can turn at least some of those nos into yeses.

DON'T BE NEGATIVE. If you've been saying no to the toddler all day, don't be shocked when it comes right back at you. Find other ways to get your point across. Instead of saying no when he asks for a biscuit before supper, say, 'Let's have some delicious veggies and dip instead.'

ASK THE RIGHT WAY. If you ask questions that can be answered only with a yes or a no, you'll get a no every time. So be clever. Instead of asking, 'Do you want to take a bath?' ask 'Do you want to take your duck or your doll into the bath with you?'

GIVE IN OCCASIONALLY. There's nothing wrong with letting a toddler have her way sometimes. If you're planning on leaving the park to go home for lunch but she's begging for more sandbox time, give in and stay for 10 more minutes. (But don't let 10 become 30, or you've lost all your authority, which isn't the idea at all. And never give in to a tantrum.)

WINNING OVER WHINING

Forget crying – even screaming. No sound is harder on the ears than a toddler's whine. But there are ways to tone it down – without reaching for a pair of earplugs. The best plan is to stop this common behaviour before it gets a chance to start.

LISTEN UP. Many toddlers whine when they've been trying unsuccessfully to get attention. So always try to respond the first time. If you're in the middle of

toddler time

TRICKS OF THE TRADE

Toddlers are slowcoaches by nature. That's because they're busy doing things that are a lot more interesting than getting to the market or being on time to nursery. For a toddler, rushing out the door means she won't be able to kiss her stuffed frog good-bye or finish her block castle. Hurrying down the block means she won't get to watch the ants cross the sidewalk or look in the toy shop window.

The best way to deal with toddler time is to build in extra time. And check out the tips on page 158 for dealing with a dawdling infant school child; you may be able to adapt some of them for younger children.

something, turn to the child and say, 'I hear you, but I can't talk to you right now. Please give me a few minutes to finish what I'm doing.'

BEAT BOREDOM. Bored toddlers are whiny toddlers. Step in with a song, an activity or an outing before the whining starts.

STOP THE CAUSE. If you know the toddler always whines when she's hungry, make sure she's not going too long between meals and snacks. If she whines when she's tired, she may need a longer nap or some downtime during the day.

DON'T GIVE IN. Never give a toddler something he's whined for. Instead, calmly request that he ask for what he wants in a normal voice. Say, 'I know you asked me for something just now, but I couldn't understand what it was because you were whining. Please ask me again in a normal voice.'

THE AT-HOME PARENT

Q *'The family I work for has a work-at-home mum. Too often during the day, the two-year-old runs to his mother when she's trying to work. I find it hard to keep him busy with me when he knows his mum is only steps away.'*

A It's hard on a young child when Mum is so near and yet so far. In order for both you and Mum to get your jobs done, you'll have to join forces to come up with a solution. For instance, it might help if she kept her door closed when she's working. Even a young child can understand that a closed door means 'stay out' and an open door 'come in'. Or, if the child knows his colours, you can use a red sign and a green sign to give 'stop' and 'go' signals. It would also help if Mum took her breaks at the same times each day – and avoided frequent visits to the kitchen or walks through the playroom. Better still, she could take her breaks when you're out with

the child (if Mum is out of sight, she may stay out of mind). It might also be helpful to plan more trips or play sessions outside the home.

Do keep in mind, however, that some parents choose to work from home just so they can spend more time with their children. If this is true in your case, work with Mum to balance your need to babysit effectively and her need to be with her child. A consistent schedule that builds in periods of 'Mum time' every day (15 minutes after lunch, 10 before nap) may help.

an ounce of prevention

A certain number of tantrums (and whining, and biting, and hitting) comes with the toddler territory. But you can prevent many of the less desirable toddler behaviours by avoiding these triggers:

TRICKS OF THE TRADE

- **FATIGUE.** Don't care for those meltdowns in the frozen foods section? Be sure to do the shopping *after* naptime – not before.

- **HUNGER.** A hungry toddler is never a cooperative one. Don't wait for the cookie to start crumbling before you offer a healthy snack.

- **BOREDOM.** A toddler who has nothing else to do is more likely to pitch a fit. For calmer trips to the supermarket, for instance, keep him busy from the moment you walk in the door: have him drop the cereal box into the cart, engage him in a search for anything circle-shaped, play 'I Spy' (see page 86) or sing a favourite song.

THE 6 P.M. MELTDOWN

Q *'The toddler I look after is happy all day. But when her parents come home, she completely melts down. I'm afraid the parents will think their daughter is unhappy all day with me and that I'm doing something wrong.'*

A Children often save their true-blue colours for their parents, so it's not unusual for meltdowns to occur the moment that key turns in the front door. (The fact that parents come home at the time of day when children are generally at their crankiest doesn't help the situation, either.) Mum and Dad are almost certainly aware that this is normal behaviour and are very unlikely to blame it on your care. You can help to ensure a happier homecoming each night, though. See page 12.

TAMING THOSE TANTRUMS

They're not called the 'terrible twos' for nothing. Tantrums (fits of anger, screaming, lie-down-on-the-floor stubbornness) are a normal fact of toddler life. Toddlers who throw tantrums aren't being bad – they're just being, well, toddlers.

The best way to deal with tantrums is to prevent them. But when there's no stopping a tantrum, you can try some of these coping tips:

STAY CALM. The more out of control the child, the more in control you need to be. Without losing your cool, get down to the toddler's eye level, speak softly and help him calm down.

DON'T PUNISH. A tantrum is normal toddler behaviour, so no need to punish.

DON'T ARGUE. You can't reason with an out-of-control toddler. It's tempting to try, but save your breath – it won't work.

MAKE SURE NO ONE GETS HURT. A kicking, flailing child can hurt herself or others, so move her to a safe location.

TRY A HUG. For some toddlers, a giant bear hug is calming. Keep in mind, though, that this approach doesn't work for all children – some will just get angrier if they're hugged.

BE SILLY. Getting the giggles going can often stop the screaming. If the toddler is refusing to wear his jacket, put it on the dog; if he's resisting the flannel, drape it over your head.

DISTRACT. Toddlers are easily distracted, so bring out a favourite book or toy, or turn on the music and start dancing. She might get caught up in a new activity and forget why she was upset to begin with. And don't make the mistake of reminding her!

TRY IGNORING IT. A toddler who finds that there's no audience for his tantrums might decide they're not worth staging. Go about your business without paying attention (but make sure he's safe and don't walk out of the room).

NEVER GIVE IN. Here's the message you send to a toddler when you cave in to a tantrum: *The best way to get what I want is to scream for it.*

BITING (AND HITTING, AND PINCHING . . .)

Don't be shocked if a toddler bites the hand that feeds her (and hugs her and plays with her). When toddlers get angry, they often can't express their anger in words, so they turn to something physical like biting or hitting. But even though biting (like hitting, or pinching, or pushing) is normal and common, it should be nipped in the bud. Here's what you can do:

STOP IT. Step in right away and say firmly, 'Don't bite.' If the biting or hitting is directed at other children, quickly prevent the child from hurting anyone. Comfort the victim promptly (which will also send the signal that biting isn't the way to get attention), and use first aid if the bite has broken the skin (wash with warm soapy water).

DON'T LAUGH. An unexpected nip or even a slap from an angry toddler can seem cute. But laughter invites a repeat performance.

DON'T BITE OR HIT BACK. This will only teach him that it's okay to bite or hit.

HELP HER USE WORDS. Have her practice saying, 'I'm mad', instead of biting or hitting.

DON'T PULL THOSE TRIGGERS. You know what they are. Being overtired, hungry or bored can make a toddler more likely to bite, slap, hit, pinch, push . . . you name it.

MOVE ON. Once you've let the toddler know that biting isn't acceptable, move on to another activity.

SHARE AND SHARE ALIKE

As far as toddlers are concerned, there's no such thing as 'yours' or 'ours' – only 'mine'. Grabbing toys or refusing to share isn't just typical behaviour; it's completely normal – and not a sign of selfishness. Still, you can help teach a young child to share.

MAKE IT EASY. When children have a lot of toys to choose from, they will be more likely to share (especially if there's more than one of a certain type of toy, like dolls or trucks). Or put out toys or activities (big puzzles, a giant bucket of crayons) that toddlers can use or do together.

PROTECT SPECIAL TOYS. Allowing a toddler to have a toy (or favourite blanket) all to herself may make her more open to sharing other things. You can also ask her to put away one special toy before friends come round to play so no one can touch it.

DISTRACT. If you see him lunging for the toy airplane another child is playing with, distract him by offering him another special toy or activity.

TEACH BUT DON'T PREACH. Talk to her about what ownership means. Explain that the truck is her friend's, the same way the stuffed animal belongs to her, and that the swings at the playground belong to everyone.

don't push

How would you like it if someone made you share your car or your favourite necklace? Well, if you think about it, a toddler's toys are just as valuable to her. So encourage sharing, but never force it. Instead, let the child know that you understand how hard sharing is.

Also talk about the emotions she feels when she has to share. Say, 'I know you're sad that you gave up the teddy bear, but Jason really loves that teddy and wants to give it a hug. You'll get another turn soon.'

ENCOURAGE TRADES. Suggest that the toddlers trade toys so that they learn how to share without being left empty-handed.

SET A BUZZER. Taking turns is easier if the buzzer decides when one child's turn is up and someone else's turn begins.

LEAD BY EXAMPLE. Share with the child – and point out what you're doing when you do it. Say, 'This is my sandwich, but I like sharing so I'll give you a piece.'

Also practise taking turns when you're alone with him (you flip one page of a book, then he flips the next, for instance). He'll soon learn that taking turns is fun.

CHEER SHARES. Whenever you see a child being generous, offer praise: 'I like the way you shared. It made Sara so happy!'

PUT IT AWAY. If there's a dispute over a toy and neither toddler agrees to take turns with it, put it away until both children calm down and agree to share.

MINDING THOSE MANNERS

Turning a toddler into Miss or Mr Manners will take some time, but it can be done. Here are a few simple things you can do to help teach a toddler those all-important p's and q's:

BE A MODEL OF MANNERS. The best way to teach a child to be polite is to be polite yourself. Use 'please', 'thank you' and 'excuse me' regularly during the day – even when talking to the toddler.

BE THAT LITTLE VOICE. Remind the toddler to use 'please' when he asks for something, and 'thank you' when he gets it (or 'no, thank you' when he's offered something he doesn't want). When he forgets, use the line that parents have used for generations: 'What's the magic word?' Also help teach the toddler how to say hello, good-bye and 'thank you for having me' when visiting, and to say 'excuse me' when someone's in his way, when he wants to get someone's attention (or he interrupts some-one) or when he burps. Soon all those phrases will become sec-ond nature.

NOTICE GOOD MANNERS. Noth-ing works better than a pat on the back. Point out how happy you are that the toddler said all her pleases and thank-yous, or that she said 'Excuse me' when you were talking to a friend and she needed help with the potty.

never shake a toddler

SAFE AND SOUND

Just as you must never shake a baby, you must never shake a toddler – ever. Shaking can cause serious eye and/or brain dam-age in babies and young children. It can even kill them. If you feel that you're out of control, give yourself a time-out: sit down, count to 10, blow off steam, or do whatever it takes to calm yourself down. Then go back to the toddler and deal with the problem – calmly and without force.

TODDLERS AND TRANSITIONS

Can't pry those little fingers off your leg at preschool dropoff? You're not alone. Many toddlers have trouble with transitions, but you can help make the breaks easier.

BRING SOME COMFORT ALONG. A comfort object from home (a beloved blanket, a stuffed animal, a favourite toy) can ease the transition from home to school. If the school won't let teddy stay, put it away in his backpack and tell him it will be there waiting when school is over.

EMPHASIZE THE POSITIVE. Instead of telling him not to cry, remind the toddler about how much fun he has at school.

HAVE A TOUR. Before you leave, let the toddler take you on a tour around the classroom. This will give her a sense of pride and ownership in her school.

GET THE TEACHER ON YOUR SIDE. Come up with a game plan with the teacher. She can help ease the separation by getting the child involved in an activity.

BE ON TIME. Part of the toddler's fear is that he'll be left at school. Don't keep him waiting when

did you know?

Getting from A to B – whether A is the playground and B is home, or A is home and B is preschool – is tough on most toddlers. That's why it helps to have a friend along for the ride. For many toddlers, that friend is a 'transitional object' – a stuffed animal, special blanket, dummy or other treasured and familiar item that makes change easier to handle.

school is over. It's much better for you to wait than the other way around.

DISCIPLINING A TODDLER

Toddlers have a lot to learn about *everything*, but especially about right, wrong, and the difference between the two. And they count on those who care for them to care enough to teach them that difference. In fact, good discipline isn't about pun-ishment, it's about teaching: Why it's wrong to hit, and why it's right to play nicely. Wrong to throw the ball in the house after you've been told not to, but right to wait until you get to the play-ground. Wrong to colour on walls, right to colour on paper. Good discipline doesn't just help children learn – it helps them feel secure and loved.

Be sure you're clear on how the parents expect you to handle misbehaving. Here are some pos-sible options:

no pulling, please

The toddler is staging a sit-down strike in the middle of the pavement? Or dawdling on the way to school (for a change)? Feel like a firm tug on the arm might be just the thing to get him going again? Don't do it. One of the most common, yet preventable, injuries to children under age five is 'nursemaid's elbow', which occurs when an adult (not neces-sarily a nursemaid) abruptly pulls a toddler's arm or drags him by the arm, causing the elbow (or sometimes the shoulder) to dislocate, or 'pop' out of its socket. Even swinging a child by the arms (which kids usually love) can result in a dislocation.

To avoid such an injury, always pick up a child under the armpits, don't swing him by the wrists and never pull or jerk his arms – in play or in anger. If you feel a dislocation injury may have occurred, get the child to the doctor as soon as possible.

SAFE AND SOUND

choose your battles

TRICKS OF THE TRADE

You can fight with a toddler over every detail – what he wears, what she eats. But you'll get tired, and the toddler will become less cooperative. Instead, save your battles for issues that really matter – like the rules parents expect to be followed and want enforced. After all, a child who has control over little things won't be as likely to fight over the big ones.

DISTRACTION. Take the child away from the crime scene. It's win-win, and it works. If the one-year-old is turning the TV on and off for fun, remove her to another room and get her involved in another activity.

DISCIPLINE THAT FITS THE CRIME. She's been warned to colour only on paper, not on the table. She colours on the table once again. *Discipline:* The crayons are taken away for the afternoon. Or, he's been told not to throw the truck. He throws the truck. *Discipline:* The truck is off-limits all day.

NATURAL CONSEQUENCES. You told her not to drop the cracker on the ground. She drops the cracker in a puddle on purpose. The natural consequence: no cracker to eat (and don't give her another one, or there goes the teaching moment!).

POSITIVE REINFORCEMENT. Pointing out good behaviour or patting a child on the back for remembering the rules is the best way to encourage repeat good behaviour.

TIME OUT. Though not useful for teaching, time-outs do give the toddler a chance to calm down when he's having a hard time controlling his behaviour. Follow the parents' guidelines for time-outs (and see pages 161–62 for more on time-outs).

discipline checklist

DO   DON'T

☑ **DO FOLLOW ALL THE PARENTS' RULES.** Setting the discipline rules and the limits in the house is the parents' job. Your job is to make sure you follow those directions, even if you don't always agree – or if you do things differently at home.

☑ **DO BE CONSISTENT.** Make sure your rules are the same as the parents' rules – and that you enforce them consistently so the child doesn't get confused. It's very unsettling when the rules are always changing.

☑ **DO FOCUS ON THE BEHAVIOUR, NOT THE CHILD.** There are no 'bad' toddlers – just bad behaviour. When a child spills his juice on purpose, don't call him a 'bad boy'; instead, explain that juice is for drinking and that spilling on purpose is unacceptable, and then have him help clean up the mess.

☒ **DON'T WITHHOLD AFFECTION.** Never let a child think love comes with strings attached ('You spilled all the milk on the floor, so I won't give you a hug'). Rejection will only make her sad – it won't help her learn from her mistake.

☒ **DON'T HIT.** Ever. Spanking only teaches that violence is okay and that big people can beat up little people; it doesn't teach right from wrong. Also, never ever shake a child.

☒ **DON'T LECTURE.** Toddlers are too young to listen to long lists of reasons why a behaviour is bad. Your lectures will sail right over that little head. For best results, keep it short and sweet to get your point across effectively: 'Please don't bite. Biting hurts.' Or, 'If you throw your truck, you might break it.'

DO	DON'T
☑ **DO GIVE ATTENTION.** Sometimes a toddler misbehaves because she wants to get your attention, and even negative attention (you end up yelling at her for tearing pages out of her book) is better than being ignored. Give her what she's craving before she uses bad behavior to get it.	☒ **DON'T EXPECT RESULTS ALL THE TIME.** Toddlers have short memories and limited control over their impulses. Just because you told the child twice not to touch the TV doesn't mean she won't touch it a third time. Expect to teach the same lessons over and over again before they start to sink in.
☑ **DO BE POSITIVE.** Always try to 'catch' a toddler being good – there's no better way to encourage more of the same. Praise good behaviour – give a hug after he helps you clean up the toys, or say, 'I'm so proud that you shared at play group today.'	☒ **DON'T LOSE CONTROL.** Knowing that the adults around them are always in control makes toddlers feel more secure. Besides, you're more likely to deliver effective discipline when you're calm.
☑ **DO TAILOR THE DISCIPLINE.** What works for one child may not work for another. It may not work for two children in the same family, or even for the same child on two different days. Each toddler is an individual, and you'll need to adapt your methods of discipline to the child in your care.	☒ **DON'T EXPECT TOO MUCH.** Keep your expectations about the toddler's behaviour age-appropriate. Don't discipline a toddler for a behaviour he's not developmentally ready to control. (For instance, a 14-month-old isn't mature enough to know that pulling chocolate off the shelf in a store is wrong; a 20-month-old can't be expected to remember to put her toys away.)

4 to 6 years

A lot more levelheaded than toddlers, four- to six-year-old are less negative, less willful, less likely to throw a tantrum. But that doesn't mean they're putty in your hands. If anything, they're more interested in testing limits – theirs and yours – than ever before. 'Let me do it myself' is a favourite phrase, as is 'I won't' – and 'You can't make me.' As they become more and more independent, this age group enjoys making decisions for themselves and sometimes gets a little carried away in its take-charge behaviour (bossy, anyone?). Yet they're loads of fun to be with – as long as you know what to expect.

THE LYING GAME

Though famous as fibbers, young children don't tell fibs to be 'bad'. They've figured out that lying is a great way to have some control over the adults (and children) around them – and to get out of trouble fast. Your job is to remind them that honesty is the best policy.

BE HONEST YOURSELF. Children learn best through the example of adults around them. Also, if the child can trust you, he'll be less likely to lie.

DON'T PLAY DETECTIVE. Don't ask questions that set up the child to lie. If you notice she coloured on the wall with a crayon, don't ask, 'Did you colour all over the playroom wall?' (which you already know). Instead, say, 'I'm disappointed that you used a crayon on the wall instead of on paper.'

FOCUS ON A SOLUTION. Instead of placing blame, help her find a solution. Say, 'Now that there's crayon all over the wall, how do you think we can fix it?' Have her help clean up the mess.

DON'T FORCE HIM TO LIE. If you overreact to a misdeed, he'll be more likely to lie about it – and about his next mistake.

REINFORCE THE TRUTH. When she's 'fessed up, let her know that you're happy about his honesty. Then discipline as directed by the parents.

A WINNING ATTITUDE ABOUT LOSING

Young children love to play games – as long as they win. Since they haven't yet learned how to deal with disappointment, you can help teach how to lose gracefully by:

BEING A GOOD LOSER. When you lose, show the child by example how to congratulate the winner and accept defeat.

PRAISING A GOOD WINNER – or a loser who doesn't throw a fit.

NOT FIXING THE GAME. Don't let the child win all the time just to avoid a scene. Instead, play the game fairly. If you win, say, 'I know it's hard to see me win, but sometimes I win and sometimes I lose. We're playing to have fun. I like playing with you, even when I lose.'

EMPHASIZING EFFORT OVER OUTCOME. Teach that old-time favourite: 'It's not whether you win or lose, it's how you play the game.' Reinforce that motto during games by saying, 'Wow, you're playing such a great game.' Don't say much when the game is over (other than 'Good game, let's play again'), whether the child wins or loses.

TOILET HUMOUR

Young children are budding comedians. They love a good (or usually bad) joke. And top on their list of things that get the giggles going (right above knock-knock jokes) is toilet humour. So don't be surprised if the Reception school child in your life comes up with a routine of pee and poo jokes to keep you entertained (or horrified).

coping with a dawdler

Young children march to a dawdling drummer. The challenge for you is to actually get where you need to go on time, without resorting to arm-pulling or screaming matches. Here are some tips to get a dawdler going:

■ **TELL WHAT'S COMING NEXT.** Motivate the child by letting him know what's next on the day's agenda. Say, 'After you brush your teeth, we'll put your shoes and raincoat on.'

TRICKS OF THE TRADE

■ **PLAY IT UP.** Make a game out of the tasks that need to be done before you go. Say, 'Let's see if you can finish brushing your teeth by the time I count to twenty.' Play musical dressing: 'See if you can finish putting your clothes on before the song stops.'

■ **ASK FOR HELP.** This will focus the child on the job at hand while making him feel like a big helper, which every child of this age group wants to be. Say, 'We're running late, so please bring me your shoes from the closet and your lunch box from the refrigerator. That will be a big help.'

■ **REMOVE DISTRACTIONS.** Make sure the TV is off and that toys are put away. Little minds have a way of wandering.

■ **BUILD IN EXTRA TIME.** If you know it will take the child 10 minutes to get out the door, start preparing for departure 15 minutes early.

■ **MAKE A CHART.** Help the child feel proud of her accomplishments. She can check off that she's brushed her teeth, combed her hair, put on her clothes, eaten her breakfast and so on. Stickers will motivate even more.

■ **BE PATIENT.** You'll *need* to be if you're caring for young children!

Luckily, you can minimize the amount of toilet humour that leaves the bathroom.

AVOID OVERREACTING. Comedians rarely repeat a joke that doesn't get a reaction. If toilet humour doesn't get a rise from the audience (you), it will have lost much of its appeal.

SET LIMITS ON TOILET HUMOUR when out in public. Tell the child, 'It's not polite to say those words in the playground. People don't like it.'

OFFER OTHER WAYS TO BE FUNNY. Come up with your own knock-knock jokes or get a book of jokes to read together.

PRIVATE TIME

Once the nappies are off (and sometimes before), older toddlers and school-age children are quick to discover that what lies beneath is quite interesting – and can be fun to touch. Self-touching is completely normal and nothing to make a child feel ashamed about. At the same time, it's important for a child to learn that touching those private parts is something that should be done only in private. When you see the child exploring under his pants, remind him to go to his room or the bathroom to do it. (Or follow the parents' rules about self-touching.)

Curiosity isn't limited to a child's own body, of course. Young children also want to discover

did you know?

Four- to six-year-olds are just beginning to understand how the world around them works. That's why they find it so funny when things aren't the way they're supposed to be. A picture of a man walking a fish instead of a dog, or the sight of a monkey dressed up like a baby, or a song made up of nonsense words will have this age group rolling with laughter.

what's under their friends' clothes. So don't be surprised if you walk into the child's bedroom to find two naked (and giggling) four-year-olds. How to handle such a situation? Don't overreact or embarrass the children. Simply ask them (as calmly as you can) to put their clothes back on. Then quickly direct them to a new (and less revealing) game.

Once the play session is over, gently remind the child that private parts are private and not to be shared with anyone. Don't make him ashamed about a natural curiosity or about his body. Calmly mention the incident to the parents when they get home (but not in front of the child).

DISCIPLINING A YOUNG CHILD

The job of disciplining may be tougher now that the child's older (and bigger!), but at least you have more effective ways to get the job done. Use only the methods that the parents approve of and use themselves;

otherwise, discipline will be confusing. And always remember the object of the disciplining game: to teach right from wrong and improve behaviour.

CONSEQUENCES. When possible, make the consequences fit the crime. If a six-year-old won't stop throwing his ball against the wall, don't let him play with the ball for a day or two. Another effective way to use consequences is to temporarily take away a privilege (like watching TV).

GUIDANCE. Often, the best way to deal with a young child defiance ('I'm not going to brush my teeth!') is to ask only once. If that doesn't get results, take the child by the hand and guide him until the task is completed. Guidance lets a child know that you expect to be listened to when you ask, not whenever he feels like listening to you. (Always guide firmly but calmly – never violently.)

DISCUSSION. This age group is old enough to begin having talks about what is right and what is wrong:

- Point out examples of right and wrong whenever you can (two children playing nicely in the sandbox, for example, or two children throwing sand at each other).

- Talk about the child's misbehaviour and about ways that she feels she might improve it. ('You didn't share your Polly doll, and then Olivia got upset. What should you have done instead?')

- Get the child's suggestions on what to do after he misbehaves. ('You threw the truck at your brother, and now he's crying. What can you do to make him feel better?'). But don't put the job of disciplining (or choosing a discipline) in the child's hands. Some jobs are best left to grown-ups.

REINFORCEMENT. It still holds true: the best way to get good behaviour is to point it out whenever you see it.

TIME-OUTS. Although children in their early school years are more in control than toddlers, they still sometimes need a chance to settle down. Time-outs can quickly help a frustrated or angry child cope with negative feelings and regain self-control, but they should be used infrequently and only right after the child has misbehaved (not an hour later when you get home from a play session). A time-out should last about one minute per age of the child (or until she's calm, whichever comes first). Set a timer to let you and the child know when it's over.

To make a time-out effective, be sure to keep these important tips in mind:

- Keep your cool. You can't teach a child to be calm when you're not. If you're upset, take a time-out for yourself, too.

- Be businesslike. If you have to carry the child to the time-out area, be sure she's facing outward in your arms, not towards you (this might seem like a hug and could send the wrong message).

■ Be flexible. If a five-year-old has calmed down before his five minutes are up, let him leave the time-out. Remember, the purpose of a time-out is to allow the child to settle down. Once that goal is reached, there's no reason to continue. Time-outs should not be used as punishment.

■ When it's over, it's over. Once the child is calm, begin with a clean slate. Avoid lecturing on the bad behaviour.

TIME-OUT TROUBLE

Q *'The parents have asked me to use time-outs when their five-year-old misbehaves, but I can't seem to make them work.'*

A Time-outs can work well if they're used only when a child has lost control. If they're used for every single behaviour slip (he dumps his cereal, you give him a time-out; he refuses to leave the playground, you give him a time-out; he says a bad word, you give him a time-out), they lose their effectiveness. Talk to the parents, and ask if you can use other discipline tools as well.

EMPTY THREATS ARE JUST THAT – EMPTY!

Imagine this scene: it's the end of a long day and you're trying (for the 10th time) to get the child in your care to help clean up the toys. You're tired and you say, without thinking, 'If you don't help me clean up these toys, I'm going to throw them all in the bin.' But the child continues to ignore you.

Now what? Both you and the child know you won't throw out the toys, but you've played your hand. The child doesn't lift a finger, and you end up cleaning the room yourself.

Instead, use other strategies that help you both win. Say, 'Let's see who can pick up the most blocks', or 'If we finish cleaning up this room before the timer goes off, we can go outside to play.'

When you do use threats, use real threats that you can (and will) follow through on, such as 'If you don't help me clean up the room today, you won't be able to play with your favourite toy tomorrow.'

STICKING TO THE RULES

Q *'The parents have established certain house rules, but sometimes they bend those rules and give in to the child. This makes it a lot harder for me to enforce the rules with her. Should I say something to them?'*

A Life is confusing when the rules are always changing – especially if you're a young child. So for her sake – and yours – set up a conference with the parents and lay out your concerns. Explain in a really nice way that inconsistent rules are hard to enforce. Together, try to come up with a list of fair, age-appropriate rules that you can all live with – and stick with. Do keep in mind, though, that it's impossible for all care providers (parents, nannies, grandparents) to always be exactly on the same page of the rulebook. As long as the most important rules are enforced consistently, the child will know what's expected of her and will (at least most of the time) behave accordingly.

give a time-in

TRICKS OF THE TRADE

To make the most of a time-out, don't forget to use its important partner: the time-in. It's always easy to pay attention to bad behaviour. What's often hard is noticing good behaviour. So double up on your efforts to pay attention to it. Say, 'You're playing by yourself so nicely,' or 'You're using your fork very well,' or 'Great idea, you're really using your head.' Throughout the day, give the child a brief hug or a thumbs-up, pat her arm, high-five her. The goal is not to interrupt what the child is doing, but to reinforce what she's doing. A child who feels good about good behaviour will want to do it more often.

caring for siblings

Whether you're caring for two kids under three, an older sibling who's at school most of the day and an infant at home, a set of twins or a toddler who's just about to become an older sibling, having more than one child on your hands means you have your hands full. Fortunately, when it comes to kids, the more the merrier (if not the easier). All you have to do is get really good at juggling.

the sibling scoop

A NEW BABY IN THE HOUSE

Has the stork paid a visit to the home you work in? If so, here's how to help the big sister or brother make that tricky transition from only (or younger) child to older sibling.

GIVE A TITLE. Make the child your 'assistant' and put her in charge of simple, age-appropriate tasks such as bringing you the baby's nappy, helping you get the bottle from the refrigerator or even giving the bottle to the baby (with help, of course).

GIVE ATTENTION. Be sure not to shower all your attention on the new baby. While Mum and Dad are home, focus on the older child, especially when visitors come to coo over the new baby.

GIVE A BREAK. Be understanding. Expect the child to act out or even regress (by acting like a baby himself). It's natural to be

getting ready for a new baby

TRICKS OF THE TRADE

To help prepare the soon-to-be big brother or sister for the new sibling's arrival, give the real scoop on babies. Read books about newborns that tell it like it is (such as *What to Expect® When the New Baby Comes Home*). Explain what new babies are really like (that they don't do much more than eat, sleep, cry and poo, and that they're not ready to play with yet); find pictures of the child as a new baby (and if you were around then, share some baby stories); and introduce the child to other babies (in the park or at a friend's house).

protecting the new baby

SAFE AND SOUND

Even a toddler who's excited about the new baby may show that excitement a little too energetically. Loving hugs can quickly turn into harder pokes and rougher probing (especially if the older child is looking for a way to express some mixed feelings). So never allow a child under the age of five to be alone in the same room with the baby, and be sure to protect the newborn by teaching the older sibling to be gentle and 'make nice'. (Take the child's hand and brush it gently against your skin to show how.) Also ask the parents before allowing an older sibling to hold or carry the baby.

resentful when the new baby attracts everyone's attention.

GIVE BENEFITS. Point out the perks of being 'big'. Little babies can't eat peanut butter sandwiches or drink from a cup. They can't have friends over or pump their legs on a swing. Little babies can't colour with crayons, make collages or paint pictures to give to Mummy and Daddy. And they can't sit on your lap and listen to a story.

GIVE PRAISE. Congratulate the child for acting 'grown up'. Play up the 'big brother' or 'big sister' angle. Before long, older siblings begin to see that they get more attention by acting big than by acting like a baby.

R-E-S-P-E-C-T

One way to teach siblings how to respect one another's need for space is by enforcing the family's privacy rules.

■ Teach children to knock first and ask to be let in, rather than barging in unannounced.

■ Allow each child to have personal toys in addition to family toys. Don't force siblings to share personal toys, but always praise them when they do. Encourage borrowing, too, but make sure they always ask before they take.

■ Let each sibling have play time with his or her friends only; keep younger siblings away so they don't spoil the fun.

JUGGLING NAPTIMES

Q '*I take care of a baby and a three-year-old with very different sleeping patterns. One is always sleeping when the other wants to play. How do I juggle naptimes?*'

A Life with more than one child is always a juggling act – an act that usually leaves the care provider with little time to call her own. That's the downside to different naptimes, but there's an upside, too: Each child gets to have special one-on-one time with you.

The tricky part of the one-nap-now, other-nap-then routine will be keeping the three-year-old happy *and* quiet during the baby's naptime. You might try scheduling quieter activities for those times (finger painting or baking cakes or making play dough). And don't forget to remind the toddler that the 'special time' will last longer if she remembers to use her quiet voice while baby is napping.

---

if it's tuesday, it must be piano lessons...

TRICKS OF THE TRADE

Siblings often have competing activities and needs. The Reception school child may have a piano lesson at the same time the toddler has a play session at the same time the baby needs a nap. Be sure to plan each child's schedule in advance with the parents and figure out how they want you to deal with conflicting schedules. And write it all down on a calendar to help you keep track!

NANNY SHARING

Q *'I've been caring for two children from two different families at the same time. I know it's not the same as sitting for siblings, but frankly, I think it's even more difficult. Sometimes I find it really hard to balance the needs of one family with those of the other.'*

A Caring for one child is sometimes tough enough. Add another child and another family, and the challenges have a way of doubling – or even tripling! Still, there are many advantages to nanny sharing – both for you and for the two families – that can make those extra challenges well worth your while. But for the arrangement to work, everyone needs to be on the same page when it comes to most childcare issues – from what foods can and cannot be served to how discipline should be handled. For best results, sit down with both sets of parents and work out all sharing issues, getting policies that everybody can live with in writing if possible. Monthly group meetings can be used to iron out problems and issues that come up along the way, as well as to update ground rules as the children grow.

DIFFERENT AGES, DIFFERENT NEEDS

It isn't easy keeping up with the needs of more than one child, especially when they're different ages. The one-year-old wants to play with a shape sorter, while her older brother wants to play with Lego (and all those tiny pieces that can end up in the baby's mouth). Big sister wants to go to the big swings in the playground, but the baby needs to stay on the baby swings. The three-year-old on the tricycle can't catch up with his six-year-old sister on the two-wheeler. Keep these tips in mind when trying to meet the needs of siblings of all ages:

TEACH PATIENCE. Younger siblings almost always love to play with older siblings, but older siblings often don't feel the same way. Remind older siblings to be patient – slowing down on the bike, for instance, so the trike can catch up. Also point out how much they can teach their little siblings, and praise them when they're patient enough to do so.

sibling rivalry checklist

They happen in the best of families — fights for attention, fights over toys or over the TV. But to keep normal sibling squabbles from turning into all-out war, you'll need to step in sometimes to keep the peace.

DO

☑ **DO HELP THEM TALK IT OUT.** Let siblings express their feelings: 'Sounds like you're mad at Sam. Tell me what's making you angry, and we'll see what we can do.'

☑ **DO OFFER ADVICE.** Younger children need help in ending fights and solving problems. Teach them how to share and take turns, how to use their words and how to compromise.

☑ **DO KEEP THE RULES.** Kids need consistency, so reinforce the parents' rules (no hitting or name-calling, no taking things without asking, and so on). Don't forget to apply them equally to each child.

☑ **DO GIVE THEM SPACE.** Allowing children to have some toys (or an area of a room) that belong only to them will cut down on quarrels. Spending one-on-one time with each child will also help. Do a puzzle with the toddler when the baby naps; sing to the baby when the preschooler is playing with trucks.

DON'T

☒ **DON'T COMPARE.** Pitting one child against the other only invites jealousy. Instead, comment on the behaviour: 'I wish the two of you wouldn't yell at each other.'

☒ **DON'T TAKE SIDES.** Even if you know who started a fight, taking sides only makes things worse. Try to let children work out differences with a little help from you.

☒ **DON'T ALWAYS MAKE THINGS EQUAL.** No matter how you try to make things even, children are bound to find something that's unfair. Instead, consider each child's specific needs.

☒ **DON'T GIVE UP.** It will take time for children to learn how to get along (and remember, they may never be best buds).

☒ **DON'T FORGET TO PRAISE.** Say 'job well done' to children who solve arguments on their own. Point out good behaviour (playing nicely together) more often than bad.

CHOOSE ACTIVITIES FOR ALL AGES. Take a walk in the park – there's something in that for everyone. The baby will enjoy all the new sights and sounds, the toddler will enjoy picking up leaves and the preschooler will enjoy searching for earthworms and ants. Put on some music and let the preschooler dance and the toddler beat on a toy drum (the baby can watch).

KEEP IT SEPARATE. As much as you can try to make games and activities meet the needs of all the children in the house, older children will still need their time alone to play with 'big kid' toys and babies will still need to explore on their own with baby toys. Do be sure, however, to keep 'big kid' toys with small pieces away from children under three to avoid choking.

YOUR CHILD AT WORK

Q *'I'd like to bring my own son to work with me sometimes. Would there be any reason why my employer might say no?'*

A Well, that depends on the employer. Some parents might have no problem with you bringing along your child. They might even encourage what amounts to a built-in play session! Other parents could have definite problems with the arrangement. They might worry that you'll play favourites with your own child, that you'll tend to his needs first or that you wouldn't be able to handle the needs of both children at the same time. They might also worry about germ-spreading (your child could bring over a cold and pass it on to their child). Still other parents might be fine with your bringing your child once in a while, but not on a regular basis. You won't know unless you ask – and that's exactly what you should do. Be specific about how often you'd like to bring your child and reassuring about the priority care their child will receive while you're on the job.

SAYING GOOD-BYE

Q *'I'm moving away, so I have to leave my nannying job. I've developed such a strong relationship with the children I take care of that I'm afraid saying good-bye will be hard for all of us.'*

A If you're the only nanny the children have known (or remember knowing), or if you've been with the family for a long time, the bond you share is a deep one. Be careful not to break the news too abruptly – or too soon (about a week ahead for a toddler, and about two weeks ahead for an older child). Sit the children down (with the parents there for backup comfort) and let them know you're leaving. Make sure you explain why, so they don't think it's their fault (young children tend to blame themselves when something bad happens in their lives). Reassure them that even though you can't care for them anymore, you'll always care about them and you'll always be their friend. Put a positive spin on the situation – talk with excitement about the new nanny and how much fun they'll have with her. If possible, work with the new nanny for a couple of days to help the children make the transition to her care. Then, even after you've left, continue to work with the parents on the transition (disappearing suddenly from a child's life can be traumatic). Stay in touch by sending postcards or calling every once in a while (if it doesn't seem to upset the children). You might even want to stop by and say hello (with the parents' okay) before you move.

TAMING THE TELL-TALE

C hildren usually tell on each other for attention and the power it brings ('I know something you don't know'). That they may also get a sibling in trouble sweetens the pot. But tattling pits siblings against each other and can worsen rivalry. Here are some ways to avoid the tell-tale trap.

IGNORE IT. Don't give in to the attention seeker by acting on her tales. First, you'll encourage more tattling if she gets what she wants (your attention and punishment for the other child). Second, you may end up disciplining unfairly if the tattler turns out to be fibbing, which is certainly a possibility.

FOCUS ON TELLING, NOT ON TATTLING. If his report gets someone else in trouble, it's tattling. If it gets someone *out* of trouble (as when a sibling is hurt and needs your help), then it's telling – and that's okay.

smoother sibling sitting

Feel a little like the old lady in the shoe sometimes? If you have so many children around that you don't know what to do (and remember, sometimes just two can make you feel that way), keep these tips in mind:

■ **RESPECT DIFFERENCES.** Every child is different, and what works for one child may not work for another. A toddler who learns to use the potty in two weeks may have a brother who takes two years to give up nappies. A shy child may have an outgoing sibling. One sibling may be a big eater, while the other just nibbles at her plate. Treat each sibling according to his or her needs.

■ **DON'T PLAY FAVOURITES.** One child may be a piece of cake, while the other's a slice of trouble; one may have a personality that's just like yours, while the other's may clash; one child may be going through rough toddler seas, while the other never rocks the boat. It's not so easy, but never play favourites.

TRICKS OF THE TRADE

■ **DON'T COMPARE.** Telling a child that his sister was already potty-trained at his age or that his brother finishes everything on his plate at lunchtime can lead to jealousy and unhealthy competition. All brothers and sisters will compete naturally ('I can jump higher than you can'); they don't need help in that department.

■ **HELP THEM GET ALONG.** Siblings don't have to be best friends (and often won't be), but they should be encouraged to play together occasionally, support each other and respect each other. A six-year-old can play a gentle game of catch with a toddler; three- and five-year-old siblings can play with blocks together; a four-year-old can talk nicely to an 18-month-old. On the other hand, older children shouldn't be forced to play with their younger siblings all the time. And all children should have the chance to play alone – or with their friends – sometimes with no siblings allowed.

LOOK FOR THE POSITIVE. Each time a child tattles on her sibling, ask her to find two or three positive things about her sister to tell you. After a while, she'll likely decide it's too much trouble to tattle.

PROMOTE PROBLEM SOLVING. Teach children they need to problem-solve instead of tattle. Say, 'What can you do about Nicole's grabbing besides telling me about it?'

TACKLING TWINS

Double the trouble or double the fun? Caring for twins can certainly double the challenge, especially when they're infants (two crying babies, two dirty nappies, two mouths to be fed at the same time), but also as they grow up. Though some twins are the best of friends and rarely fight, others may seem to argue constantly. That's because they're at the same developmental place; they fight more because they want the same toys and crave the same amount of attention. Caring for twins means keeping all the tips on caring for siblings in mind – and then some:

TREAT THEM AS INDIVIDUALS. Even identical twins are two different people with completely different personalities. Treat them that way, rather than lumping them together. (Call them by their own names, for instance, instead of calling them 'the twins', and let them make their own choices about clothing or bedtime stories.)

GIVE THEM THEIR SPACE. Whether they're as close as two people can be or fight like kittens and puppies over everything and anything, twins need to have some things they can definitely call their own – their own toys, their own special corner in the playroom and, eventually, their own play sessions and friends.

GIVE THEM ATTENTION. All children need one-on-one attention from an adult, so be sure to spend 'alone time' with each child.

TWIN TIME

Q *'I care for the most adorable 14-month-old twins. The parents want them fed and bathed by 6 P.M. Fair enough, but some days the boys are just so uncooperative. Even getting them into the bath takes forever – and then they don't want to get out. What should I tell the parents when they come home to find the boys still splashing in the bath?'*

A Tell them the truth – something they're sure to relate to. After all, they've been parents of twins for 14 months now (struggling to get them fed and bathed on time, too). As long as you're trying your best to keep the boys on track (or at least keep them from sliding too far off track), the parents are likely to understand when you don't make that 6 P.M. deadline. Setting a buzzer to let the boys know when bathtime is over could help put you back on schedule – as could the promise of another, special activity when they come out of the tub (like lining up at the window to watch for Mummy's or Daddy's car).

◆ ◆ ◆

CHAPTER 10

Childcare basics

new at the childcare game? Or just need a refresher course on the basics? Whether you're completely clueless or a little rusty, whether you have lots to learn or only need to fill in a few blanks, this chapter's for you. From how to hold, feed and burp a baby to how to dress or potty-train a toddler, the pages that follow will give you everything you need to know to turn pro or brush up on your technique.

the first year

Even the most seasoned parent can feel a little rusty when handling a brand-new baby. These newborn basics are a good way to brush up on, well, the basics.

GIVE A LIFT

Handling a floppy newborn takes a lot of support and an extra-gentle touch. These easy how-to's will make you and baby comfortable when you lift him:

WASH YOUR HANDS. Newborns can catch colds (and other illnesses) easily, so you'll need to be careful not to pass along germs.

MAKE YOUR PRESENCE KNOWN. Before lifting, bend over close so the baby will feel safely cuddled. Whisper the baby's name or look down and smile at him so he knows what's coming.

GIVE THE BABY TIME TO ADJUST. Slip your hands under the baby's body and keep them there for a few seconds before you actually lift her up.

OFFER SUPPORT. To lift the baby, use one arm to support his bottom, and your other arm and hand to support his back, neck and head.

Support the baby while lifting.

When lifting a baby who's been playing on her tummy, slip one hand under her chin and neck and the other hand between her legs.

GET A HOLD

Try the following favourites for carrying baby.

CRADLE HOLD. A newborn can be cradled very snugly and securely in just one arm (with your hand on his bottom and your forearm supporting his back, neck and head) or in two arms for greater support.

Shoulder hold for a bigger baby.

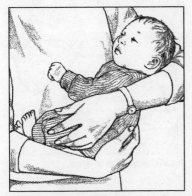

Cradle hold for a newborn.

SHOULDER HOLD. When holding a baby over your shoulder, keep one hand under her legs and buttocks and the other hand supporting her back, neck and shoulders. It's true that an older baby will probably need less neck support than a newborn does, but she'll still need plenty of back support.

FRONT CARRY. Face an older baby out, with one hand across his chest and the other hand supporting his bottom.

The front-face carry.

HIP CARRY. Hold an older baby snugly against your body with one arm, resting her bottom on your hip.

The hip carry.

DOWN YOU GO

Babies love to be carried, and they benefit from those rides in your arms. But while being a 'baby taxi' is an important part of your job, it's important to know how to make the move from your arms to the cot (or any other surface):

HOLD BABY CLOSE. As you bend over, keep the baby close, with one hand on her bottom and the other hand supporting her back, neck and head.

GIVE BABY TIME TO ADJUST. Keep your hands in place for a few moments until the baby feels the comfort and security of the mattress. Then gently slip your hands out.

Putting baby down to sleep.

AND YOU'RE DONE. A few light pats or some gentle hand pressure (depending on what seems most pleasing to the baby) will ease the transition from your arms. If the baby is awake, smile and whisper a few reassuring words ('Nighty-night, sweet girl') before making the break.

WINDING BABY'S

Because young babies eat every few hours, you'll have to do a lot of winding. See which one of these positions works best for the baby in your care.

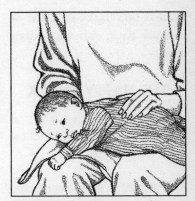

Winding baby face-down on your lap.

Winding baby against your shoulder.

OVER YOUR SHOULDER. Hold the baby firmly against your shoulder, supporting his buttocks with one hand and patting or rubbing his back with the other.

FACE-DOWN ON YOUR LAP. Turn the baby face-down on your lap, stomach over one leg, head resting on the other. Holding her

securely with one hand, pat or rub with the other.

SITTING UP. Sit the baby on your lap, head leaning forward and chest supported by your arm, making sure the baby's head

Winding baby while he's sitting up.

doesn't flop backwards. Pat or rub his back with your other hand.

THE NAPPY KNACK

Changing nappies can be quick and easy if you follow these simple steps.

BE PREPARED. Have everything you need close by, including:

- A change of clothes in case the nappy leaks (pretty likely in the early months)

- A clean nappy

- Wet wipes

- Cotton balls and warm water (for babies with sensitive skin)

- Ointment or cream (to prevent nappy rash)

for the nappy wiper

Since you'll be making many changes during the early months, you'll want to keep these changing tips in mind:

TRICKS OF THE TRADE

- Keep a nappy count to ensure that the baby is getting enough to eat and drink. Nappies that stay dry too long may mean baby is sick, so make sure you tell the parents if you see a difference in the number of nappies you're changing.

- To keep a baby boy's clothes dry, aim the penis down when you put on the nappy.

- Keep a baby boy's penis covered with a clean nappy for as much of the changing process as possible, so you, the furniture and the walls don't get sprayed!

- If you're changing a newborn and her umbilical stump is still attached, fold the nappy down to expose the raw area to air to prevent rubbing.

when the poop pops

Just when you think you've got the nappy basics down pat, the baby will stage a nappy blowout. We're talking poo down the leg, up the back and out the corners of the nappy. More common among breast-fed babies, exploding poo nappies come with child-minding territory. Sure it's gross, but if you're armed with plenty of wipes and a change of clothes (or, in extreme cases, with a baby bath already filled), baby will be clean again in no time. So hold your breath and dive in.

DISTRACT. Provide some entertainment for the baby (a rattle, a mobile, a stuffed animal, your smiling face) to keep her busy while you do the deed.

WIPE IT UP. After using the old nappy and (clean) wet wipes to clean baby's bottom (making sure you get into all the creases), lift both legs and slip the soiled nappy out and the clean one under. Be sure you clean a girl from top to bottom, not the other way around, to avoid spreading germs.

PROTECT WITH OINTMENT. Pat the baby's bottom dry with a clean washcloth or dry nappy,

apply ointment or cream and secure the clean nappy.

WASH UP. It's a dirty job – and since you're the one who's got to do it, don't forget to wash your hands after it's done (with soap and water or with a clean wet wipe).

SWADDLING MAGIC

Some newborns love to be swaddled (though not all do – ask the parents what their baby prefers). A snug wrapping is especially helpful for soothing a colicky baby and for keeping him comfortable and asleep on his back. But swaddling is best for young infants only; once the baby becomes too active and can kick the blanket off, it's time to stop wrapping.

1. Place a blanket on a flat surface, with the top corner folded down about six inches. Position the baby's shoulders on the fold of the blanket.

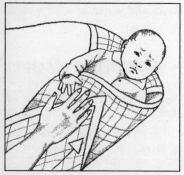

2. Take one side point of the blanket and bring it across the baby's body. Tuck the end under the baby. Bring up the bottom point of the blanket and hold it in place.

3. Bring the remaining side of the blanket over the baby and tuck under.

TEETHING TROUBLES

Baby's pearly whites usually start breaking through somewhere around six months. But it's not all smiles when teething starts. Here's how you can help a baby who's crying from teething pain:

TRY A CHEW. An ice-cold teething ring works. So does a frozen banana, though you'll have a sticky mess to clean up after.

GIVE A RUB. A clean finger rubbed against the gum can help. Some babies will cry for a moment, since the first rub hurts, but will then settle down as it brings relief.

TRY A COLD DRINK. Ice-cold water in a bottle or cup (without ice, of course) can help (if the baby is allowed to drink water). It will also replace lost fluids in a baby who's drooling by the bucketful.

TRY A PAIN RELIEVER. A baby who's really uncomfortable can be given a baby pain reliever, but ask the parents first. (Never give or rub any medicine or home remedy on the baby's gums without first getting the go-ahead.)

1 to 3 years

Never tackled a toddler before? The more tricks you have up your sleeve, the better you'll fare.

DRESSING WITHOUT STRESSING

If you haven't heard it already, you'll hear it soon and often: 'I do it myself.' You'll hear it when it's time to pour a drink, brush teeth – or get dressed. Though letting toddlers dress themselves always takes a lot longer, it's the only way they can learn this important skill. Here's how to help:

LAY OUT THE CLOTHES on a bed or floor. Line up the shoes in front of the right and left feet.

GET THE PROCESS GOING. Get the trousers onto the feet, then let the toddler pull them up. Get the arms started into the correct sleeves of the shirt, then let him finish the job.

BE PATIENT. It will take time (especially with buttons), but practice makes perfect.

BE UNDERSTANDING. If the child puts on two different-colour socks or wears his T-shirt backwards, it's okay. There's no need to correct his mistakes except for safety or social reasons.

STEP IN to help if the toddler becomes frustrated, but don't take the job over unless she asks.

a jacket to flip over

Teach an older toddler or preschooler the jacket-flip, and he'll be dressed for success in no time. It's as easy as 1-2-3-4:

TRICKS OF THE TRADE

■ Lay a jacket or coat (backside down) on the floor.

■ Have the child stand at the neck of the jacket.

■ Help the child to place his arms in the jacket while it's still on the floor.

■ Show him how to flip the jacket over his head – and bingo, the jacket is on.

GET READY TO POTTY

There's no magic age when a child's ready to graduate to a potty. All toddlers learn on their own timetable, usually between the second and third birthdays (though some master the potty a little sooner and others much later). But there's no point in starting the process until a toddler is ready. Or in pushing the process. After all, using a potty is one thing you can't force a child to do against her will. Once the parents have decided it's time for potty training, there are ways to help the process along.

■ Let the toddler go bare-bottom at home and/or in the garden. This will help him get in touch with body signals (and it'll be hard for him to miss a river trickling down his leg). Of course, you'll need to okay this with the parents first.

■ Dress the toddler in clothes that are easy to pull up and down (no dungarees, please!). Get her to practise pulling her trousers up and down by herself – to plenty of cheering!

■ Watch the toddler for those 'I gotta go' signs (squirming, grunting, pushing).

■ Never force a toddler to sit on the potty. Let him be in control and decide when he wants to sit and when it's time to get up from the potty.

■ Have potty, will travel. Let the toddler take a portable potty from room to room, so it's always close by when the urge strikes.

■ Make the potty fun. Read stories or sing a potty song while the toddler sits.

■ Let the toddler teach a doll or teddy to 'use' the potty while she learns. (A drink-and-wet doll is ideal.)

■ Be a cheering member of the potty team. When it works, give a big hug and a round of applause.

■ Small rewards (a sticker on a potty chart every time there's potty success, for instance) can work for some toddlers.

■ Don't nag or tease. Let the toddler feel good about potty training.

■ Above all, be patient and don't expect too much too soon. It takes time to learn how to use the potty. When an accident happens (and it will!), don't make a big deal. Just enlist the child in a quick cleanup, and start over again.

LATE POTTY TRAINING

Q *'I potty-trained my own children when they were under two. The boy I take care of is almost three, and his parents say he's not ready. What's going on here?'*

A There have been some changes in the potty department since your kids were little. Most experts no longer believe that children should be pushed into using the toilet at an early age; instead, they agree that it's better to wait until a child shows signs that he's ready. Research shows that a child who's ready will master the potty much more quickly than a child who's not (which means less mess for you!). While some children are ready by age two, many others aren't primed for the potty until three. Give it time, and he'll be out of nappies soon. After all, as they say, no child goes off to college in nappies.

4 to 6 years

HOLDING IT IN

Some children, even those who are old hands at the potty, continue to have trouble with bowel movements – the most common problem being that they hold them in, causing belly pain and constipation. Here are some tips to help the child go.

FIGHT BACK WITH FIBRE. Serve up more fibre to soften the stool, making a delayed bowel movement (whenever it happens) less painful. To bring on regular BMs, you can bring on:

■ Fresh and dried fruits

■ Vegetables (especially yummy with dip)

■ Fibre crackers

■ Fluids such as water and prune juice

READ BOOKS on toileting (such as *What to Expect® When You Use the Potty*) that will assure the child that bowel movements are natural and everyone has them.

GET CREATIVE TO ENCOURAGE MOVEMENT. Tell the child that there's a poo-poo party in the toilet and his poo is invited to the fun.

REINFORCE SUCCESS. Have the child help make a chart. When she has BM success, let her reward herself with a sticker.

BUT TONE IT DOWN. When there *is* success, offer praise but don't go overboard. If you make too big a deal out of it, the child may crave that attention and start the cycle (holding it in for a long time and then pooing it out to a round of applause) again.

POTTY MISHAPS

It's hard to expect a four- or even six-year-old to be a potty pro all the time. After all, young children often get so involved in an activity that they don't realize they have to use the toilet until it's too late. Or they're already asleep when they get the urge to go and never make it to the toilet at all. Accidents and bed-wetting happen, so you'll need to be armed with tips to help deal with them.

REMAIN CALM AND SUPPORTIVE. It's upsetting and embarrassing to be a big boy or girl and have an accident, so be matter-of-fact about it and simply help the child change into dry clothes. Encourage the child to use the toilet next time.

USE GENTLE REMINDERS. If you see the child getting too involved in an activity to pay attention to her toilet needs, gently ask her every hour if she needs to use the toilet. Make it a policy that everyone needs to use the toilet before leaving home (including you!). And make *her* the 'toilet police'.

TELL THE PARENTS. Let the parents know about any accidents (day or night) their child is having.

◆ ◆ ◆

CHAPTER 11

health & safety

being a childcarer is great fun, but there's a serious side to it, too. For as many as eight hours a day (sometimes even more), you're responsible for the health and safety of a child. That responsibility includes protecting a child from injuries, taking care of a child who's sick, and responding in any emergency. That's why being prepared for anything – from a bloody nose to a tumble off the slide – is such an important part of a care provider's job. Knowing what to do will help you stay calm – the key to handling any emergency well.

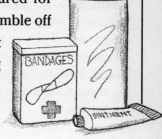

first aid — the basics

Even with your eyes constantly on them (as they should be), you can't always protect children from falls, scrapes and bruises. Keep these first-aid tips in mind when 'kissing it better' isn't sufficient.

MINOR CUTS AND SCRAPES. Wash gently with soap and water. If you're not home, you can use a wet wipe. Put on a bandage (and don't forget to add that kiss).

DEEP CUTS. Apply pressure to the cut with a clean gauze or wet cloth until bleeding stops. If a cut is deep and/or won't stop bleeding, it may need stitches, so call the parents right away. Call the doctor, too, while continuing to apply pressure.

BUMPS. Apply ice to the bump to stop the swelling. If it's a serious head bump, watch for signs of a concussion (vomiting, dizziness, loss of consciousness, eyes looking strange, sleepiness) and call the parents.

SPLINTERS. Wash the area with soap and water. If the splinter is sticking out and looks easy to remove, you can try gently pulling it out with tweezers that have been sterilized with alcohol. If you can't get it out easily and the child is not in pain, leave it in (it will probably come out on its own). Tell the parents, though, so they can check to make sure the area doesn't get infected.

BURNS. Run cool water over a minor burn for 10 minutes. Never apply ice or butter. If the burn is more serious (over a large area of the body, on the face, hands or genitals, or is oozing or starting to blister) or if the child is under one year old, call the parents and a doctor right away. If the burn is severe (the skin appears white or charred, or you can see serious injury to the deeper skin layers), call 999.

PUNCTURE WOUNDS. Wash the area in warm soapy water. Cover with a bandage. Call the parents if the wound is deep and/or bleeding a lot (remember to apply pressure) or if an object (like a pencil or nail) is still stuck in the child's skin.

EYE INJURIES. Rinse the eye with cool water if something is stuck inside (such as a speck of dirt, an eyelash or an insect). Call the parents if the eye has been poked and the child complains of more than brief pain. Call 999 if the eye has been seriously hurt, as by a puncture wound (from a pencil, for instance), and is bleeding.

MOUTH INJURIES. Clean the injury and apply ice to the area. Mouth cuts bleed a lot, so they often look worse than they are. But if bleeding continues for longer than 10 minutes, call the parents.

If a baby tooth has been knocked out, call the parents right away. If a permanent tooth has been knocked out or loosened, call the parents and a dentist immediately; keep the dislodged tooth in a cup of milk or water so the dentist can try to reimplant it.

INSECT BITES AND STINGS. Wash bites and stings with soap and water. Ask the parents ahead of time

did you know?

Most local hospitals and Red Cross branches offer classes in first aid and CPR. They probably also offer refresher CPR courses (a good idea if it's been a while since you got your certification).

TRICKS OF THE TRADE

cool as ice

Popsicles are as cool as ice, and a lot more fun for a child to suck on when he's just banged his mouth. Keep a supply in the freezer – especially if you have an active child on your hands.

call the doctor

SAFE AND SOUND

Call the doctor as the parents have directed you and also if:

- There is bleeding that won't stop after 10 minutes of pressure.

- A baby has been burned.

- An older child has a large burn over a large area of the body or on the face, hands or genitals, or if the burn is oozing or blistering.

- The child is in severe pain.

- There's a possibility of broken bones.

- The child has an extreme allergic reaction.

- The child has swallowed something sharp, such as a pin or nail, a piece of glass or a toothpick.

if you can apply anti-itch lotion. Some children are allergic (to bee stings, for instance), so check for reactions such as swelling, severe pain and/or difficult breathing. If any of these happen, call the parents and the doctor right away. Parents who know their child has an allergy will have told you what to do in case of a severe reaction. They may want you to give an injection or to call for emergency help.

HUMAN OR ANIMAL BITES. Wash the bite with warm soapy water. If the bite breaks the skin, call the parents.

NOSEBLEEDS. Sit the child down with his head bent forward and pinch both nostrils gently for 10 minutes. (Make sure the child switches to mouth breathing.) If bleeding hasn't stopped, pinch for 10 minutes more and call the parents.

FIRST AID & CPR TRAINING

Q *'I want to take a first aid and CPR course. Is it okay to ask the parents to pay for it?'*

A Most parents are more than happy to reimburse for CPR training – after all, it's a small price to pay for peace of mind – so don't hesitate to ask. But even if the parents aren't willing to pay for the course, don't let that stop you. Consider it an investment in your career.

BOO-BOO BULLETINS

Q *'The girl I care for tripped and got a bump on her head. What's the best way to tell the parents?'*

A That depends on how big the bump is and how accident-prone the child is. If it's a major bump – or if the child doesn't hurt herself very often – don't wait until the parents come home to let them know about it. Call (or e-mail) them at work, tell them exactly what happened and

how, and reassure them (that you've applied ice, that you've comforted the child, that she's doing fine). If you can't reach them, tell them what happened as soon as they arrive home. Either way, let your calm tone of voice speak for itself. (If you sound upset, the parents are likely to get upset, too – as will the child if she's within earshot.) And remember: always tell the truth.

Of course, if you're caring for a child (a new walker, say) who can't get through a morning without a half-dozen bumps or bruises, the parents probably don't need a blow-by-blow of every tumble. Unless they tell you differently, save the rundown of those falldowns for your end-of-the-day chat.

call 999

SAFE AND SOUND

Get to a phone immediately and call 999 if any of the following happen:

- The child is choking.
- The child isn't breathing or is unconscious.
- The child is bleeding severely (gushing or squirting blood) or is losing lots of blood.
- The child has a major injury such as a severe broken bone (you can see a piece of bone sticking out) or there is the possibility of a back or neck injury.
- The child has been burned over a large area of the body (as by scalding water) or a burn is causing the skin to peel.
- The child has a serious eye injury or a puncture wound to the eye (as from a pencil).

in case of emergency

CHOKING

If the child starts turning blue and making a choking sound or no sound at all, tell someone nearby to call 999. If you're alone and forget what to do, take the child to the phone and call 999. Otherwise, go through the following steps for one minute and then call 999. Then continue with rescue efforts if the child is still not breathing.

FOR INFANTS UNDER ONE YEAR

1. Position the baby. Place the baby tummy down on your arm, head lower than torso, with her chin in your hand.

2. Administer blows. With the other hand, give five forceful blows to the baby's back between the shoulders. (See illustration at right.)

3. Chest thrusts. If the object doesn't come out, turn the baby over, place him on a hard surface and, using your index and middle fingers, give four chest thrusts (about one-inch deep) over the breastbone.

4. Mouth sweep. If the baby is still choking, look in her mouth for a foreign object. If you see one, remove it with a sweep of your finger. (Don't sweep the mouth if you don't see anything, and never try to remove an object by pinching it with your finger.)

Giving back blows to a choking infant.

5. Check breathing. If the baby is not breathing, place your mouth over his mouth and nose, and give two slow breaths.

6. Repeat. Continue until the baby stops choking or until help arrives.

FOR CHILDREN OVER AGE ONE

1. Position the child. *If the child is conscious:* Stand or kneel behind the child and wrap your arms around his waist. Place your fist against the child's abdomen, slightly above the belly button. (See illustration below.)

If the child is unconscious: Place the child face up on a table or on the floor. Stand or kneel at the child's feet and place one of your hands on top of the other on the child's stomach between the belly button and the rib cage. (See illustration below.)

2. Administer thrusts. Give five quick inward-and-upward abdominal thrusts to dislodge the foreign object.

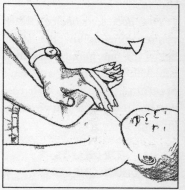

Administering thrusts to an unconscious child.

3. Mouth sweep. Remove any foreign object with a sweep of your finger.

4. Check breathing. If the child is not breathing, place your mouth over the child's mouth and give two quick breaths.

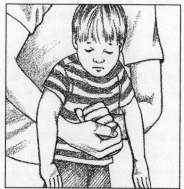

Positioning a conscious child correctly for abdominal thrusts.

5. Repeat. Continue until the child stops choking or until help arrives.

RESCUE BREATHING

If the child is not breathing but has a pulse or heartbeat, you'll need to perform rescue breathing – which hopefully you have learned in your first-aid course.

First, have someone call 999. If you're alone, follow the steps below for one minute and then call 999. If the child still isn't breathing, continue with rescue breathing after you've called for help.

Performing rescue breathing on an infant.

should rise with your breaths. (See illustration above.)

3. Continue. Continue with one breath every three seconds until the baby is able to breathe on her own or help arrives.

FOR INFANTS
UNDER ONE YEAR

1. Position the baby. Lay the baby on her back, tip her head back and lift her chin to open the airway.

2. Begin rescue breathing. Place your mouth over the baby's mouth and nose, and give two small breaths (about a second and a half each). The baby's chest

FOR CHILDREN
OVER AGE ONE

1. Position the child. Lay the child on his back, tip his head back and lift his chin to open the airway.

2. Begin rescue breathing. Pinch the child's nose closed and seal your mouth over his mouth. Give two breaths (about a second and a half each). Look for the

Performing rescue breathing on an older child.

child's chest to rise. (See illustration above.)

3. Continue. Continue with one breath every three seconds until the child is able to breathe on his own or until help arrives.

CPR

I f the child is not breathing and has no pulse or heartbeat, you'll need to perform CPR, which hopefully you have learned in your first-aid course.

First, have someone call 999. If you're alone, follow the steps below for one minute and then call 999. Continue with CPR after you've called for help.

FOR INFANTS
UNDER ONE YEAR

1. Position the baby. Lay the baby face up on a firm surface. Tilt her head back slightly and open her mouth. Place your mouth over the baby's mouth and nose, and give two small breaths, each about a second and a half in length.

2. Position your fingers. Place the tips of your third and fourth fingers in the centre of the baby's chest, about half an inch below the nipples.

3. Perform compressions. Press one-half inch to one inch into the chest five quick times, then give the baby one breath. (See illustration below.)

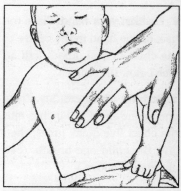

Performing chest compressions on an infant.

4. Repeat. Repeat this five-compressions-then-one-breath cycle 20 times over the next minute (100 compressions per minute). Then check for a pulse for about five seconds. Continue this process, checking for a pulse every two minutes, until you feel a pulse or help arrives.

Performing chest compressions on an older child.

FOR CHILDREN
OVER AGE ONE

1. Position the child. Lay the child face up on a firm surface. Tilt his head back slightly and open his mouth. Pinch the child's nose and seal your mouth over his mouth. Give two breaths, each about a second and a half in length.

2. Position your hand. Place the heel of one hand in the centre of the child's chest, about half an inch below the nipples.

3. Perform compressions. Press one to one-and-a-half inches into the chest five quick times, then give the child one breath. (See illustration above.)

4. Repeat. Repeat this five-compressions-then-one-breath cycle 20 times over the next minute (100 compressions per minute). Then check for a pulse for about five seconds. Continue this process, checking for a pulse every two minutes, until you feel a pulse or help arrives.

KEEPING CALM

Q *'I'm certified in CPR, but I'm worried that I'll panic in an emergency.'*

A The single most important thing you can do in an emergency is to stay calm – not only

poison control

If a child has accidentally swallowed poison, cleaning solution, medicine or anything else that might be harmful, call 999 *immediately*. (Never induce vomiting or treat the child in any other way without medical advice.) Have the bottle of poison with you when you call, and be prepared to give the child's age and weight (see the inside front cover of this book). Follow the directions given by the emergency services, and call the parents.

so you'll remember what to do, but so that you can be a source of comfort and reassurance for the child. If you become hysterical, you can be sure the child will, too.

First, take a deep breath. Remind yourself that you're prepared for an emergency. Then, quickly survey the situation; if it's life-threatening, begin first aid and call 999. While you're waiting for help, continue with first aid. And don't forget the parents. Call them as soon as you have a free hand and the child is out of danger, staying as calm as you can when reporting to them.

when the child is sick

It's inevitable. Where there are children, there are germs. And where there are germs, there are colds, runny noses, sore throats and other illnesses. The baby you care for has been pulling his ear all afternoon; by evening, it's clear he has an ear infection. The happy toddler you left yesterday evening woke up with a fever and is now coughing and miserable in bed. The preschooler is spending the day at home with a sore throat. And with the parents at work, it's up to you to help nurse the child back to health. But before you put on your white cap and get started, you'll need to know a little bit about common childhood illnesses.

FEVER

You can often tell that a child has a fever before you even get out the thermometer. His eyes are glassy, or she's been cranky all day; his body feels warmer than usual, or she's lost her always robust appetite; he's sleeping a lot more than usual, or she's got no energy.

If you suspect a fever, be sure to follow the parents' instructions for caring for a sick child. Do not give any medications or remedies without the parents' permission. If the child has a fever over 101°F and you cannot reach the parents, call the doctor before you give any medications.

TAKING A CHILD'S TEMPERATURE

For a more accurate reading than the old hand-to-the-forehead test, just follow these simple steps:

Pick the thermometer. Ask the parents which type of thermometer they prefer you to use:

handling fever seizures

SAFE AND SOUND

Occasionally, a baby with a very high fever will have a convulsion called a febrile seizure. The seizure, which usually lasts a minute or two, isn't dangerous (though it can be scary to watch, especially the first time). If the baby in your care starts to seize with a fever, lay him on his side, with his head lower than his body (propping his body slightly with a folded blanket or pillow). Remove anything from his mouth (dummy, bottle), and stay with him. After the seizure stops, call the doctor and the parents for advice.

■ *Digital thermometer.* This type of thermometer can be used to take a rectal (in the bottom), oral (in the mouth) or armpit reading (but don't use the same thermometer for oral and rectal) in about 20 to 60 seconds.

■ *Dummy thermometer.* The dummy-shaped thermometer is designed to give a mouth reading in a baby too young to use an oral thermometer.

■ *Tympanic (ear) thermometer.* Used mostly for toddlers and older children (they're less accurate in babies), ear thermometers provide a reading in just seconds. (They can be difficult to position and use correctly, so ask the parents to show you how to use one properly and efficiently.)

Calm the child down. Try to keep the child quiet for 15 minutes before taking her temperature. Crying or screaming could make the fever go up.

Take the temperature. First, distract the child by singing a favourite song or giving him a toy to hold. (If he's too young to hold a toy, put one where he can see it.) Then use one of these methods, based on the type of thermometer you're using:

■ *Rectal.* Lubricate the tip of the thermometer with Vaseline. Place the child, tummy down and bottom exposed, on your lap or changing table (for infants) or on a bed. Spread the buttocks with one hand and slip about an inch of the tip of the thermometer into the rectum, being careful not to force it. Hold the thermometer in place until it beeps.

■ *Underarm.* Move the child's top so it won't come between the thermometer and her skin, and be sure the armpit is dry. Place the tip of the thermometer well up into the armpit, and hold the arm snugly over it until it beeps.

■ *Ear.* Gently place the special tympanic thermometer into the child's ear (again, be sure to get the parents to show you how), and press the button for the reading. A toddler or older child will be distracted enough to cooperate if you say you're looking for a giraffe (or favourite cartoon character) in his ear.

■ *Oral.* Children under age five should not use an oral thermometer (other than the dummy type). For an older child, place the thermometer under the child's tongue, have him close his lips, and wait until it beeps.

READ THE THERMOMETER. The reading you'll get from a rectal temperature is the most accurate. The norm for an oral reading is 98.6° F; for a rectal reading, 99.6° F; for underarm, 97.6° F.

COMMON ILLNESSES

Just about every child (including the child in your care) will get sick at one time or another. Here's what you need to know about common illnesses:

COLD OR FLU. The symptoms of a cold or flu can include coughing, sneezing, runny nose, sore throat and low fever. Here's how you can help make a sick child feel better:

■ *Let appetite rule.* A sick child should eat as much or as little as she wants – no forcing, no withholding. And simple does it. Serve comfort foods like soup, toast, applesauce, scrambled eggs.

■ *Pour on the drinks.* Children (especially babies) should drink often when they have a cold. Older children may like to suck on ice pops.

■ *Encourage rest.* Suggest rest or extra naps to a child who's feeling more tired than usual (no need to push sleep on a sick child who's feeling energetic, though). To make breathing easier when the child is lying down, prop his head with pillows (for babies, place the pillows *under* the mattress).

■ *Medicate if needed.* If a child is running a fever and is very uncomfortable, the parents may suggest that you use infants' or children's acetaminophen (paracetamol/Calpol) or ibuprofen (Nurofen). Make sure you read the label carefully and give the right dose according to the parents' direction.

■ *Call the parents.* If fever shoots up, if a baby starts to cry uncontrollably or pulls on her ear, if an older child begins to complain of pain in the ears, jaw or neck, call the parents to let them know.

DIARRHOEA OR VOMITING. Symptoms of diarrhoea include loose, watery bowel movements and sometimes stomachache. Vomiting can also make the stomach hurt. To help:

■ *Push fluids.* A child who has diarrhoea or vomiting is losing a lot of fluids that need to be replaced. So keep those drinks coming (formula or breast milk for babies; water, diluted fruit juice, clear broth or ice pops for older children). If the child throws up the liquids, continue giving small amounts every 15 minutes, since some liquid is bound to stay down. A baby or young child who's lost a lot of fluid may need a rehydration drink (or rehydration ice pop); check with the parents.

■ *Don't push food.* Let the child's tummy be your guide at mealtime. If he's hungry, serve very bland foods (such as toast, white rice, bananas). If not, don't try to force-feed.

Remember to discuss in advance with the parents what you should do if the child gets sick in the middle of the day. Ask the parents if they want to be called if their child starts to throw up after lunch or if she's suddenly come down with a bad case of the sniffles.

HELPING THE MEDICINE GO DOWN

Some kids open up wide for medicine (especially when it tastes like strawberries); others crinkle their noses and slam their lips shut as soon as they see the jar coming their way. Still, when the child in your care needs medicine, it's your job to make sure he gets the right dose at the right time. Here are some tips that may make that job a little easier:

WRITE IT DOWN. Keep a record of the time each dose is given (tape a sheet of paper to the fridge) so both you and the parents will know when the last one was given.

STAY ON SCHEDULE. It's important to give children their medicine on time. If you'll be out of the house, take it with you (but pack it with ice if it needs to be refrigerated).

BE EXACT. Use special dosing cups, droppers, syringes or measuring spoons (not regular spoons), and be precise in your measurements.

GET IT DOWN. A sick child needs to drink every drop of her medicine, whether she likes it or not (or screams or not). If the child throws up the medicine after you've given it to her, call the parents or the doctor for advice on what to do next.

KEEP HIM UP. Make sure the child is upright when taking medicine so he doesn't choke (but never squeeze his cheeks, hold his nose or force his head back, which could cause choking).

DON'T DILUTE. Don't hide medicine in food or drink without the parents' okay. Chilling medicine (again with the parents' okay)

keep the germs away

Germs are everywhere – but that doesn't mean you have to let them get the upper hand.

SAFE
AND
SOUND

■ WASH UP. Remind the child to wash his hands when coming in from outside, before and after eating, and after going to the toilet or blowing his nose. Make sure you wash along with the child, and remember to wash up after a nappy change and before you pick up a newborn.

■ BE PREPARED. Carry wipes with you for quick cleanup when there's no soap and water.

■ COVER UP. Remind kids to turn their heads when they cough or sneeze, and to use a tissue to wipe their noses.

■ KEEP PUDDLES OFF-LIMITS. Though they're a blast to jump in, they're also full of germs, so keep those little hands out of that dirty water.

■ KEEP WELL CHILDREN AWAY FROM SICK CHILDREN. If there's one thing that children are good at sharing, it's germs.

■ KEEP TOYS CLEAN. Wash toys that other children have mouthed.

can make it taste less icky. Another trick: sucking on an ice pop can numb taste buds before taking medicine.

FINISH IT UP. Continue to administer the medication for as long as recommended by the doctor and as directed by the parents, even if the child looks and/or feels better.

SICK DAYS

Q 'If I'm feeling a little under the weather (say my nose is running and my throat hurts, but I don't have a fever), should I call in *sick? One of the parents would have to stay home from work and I would feel even worse!'*

A Talk the situation over with the parents. Chances are they won't want you to work if you're really sick. First, they won't want you bringing your germs to work with you, especially if there's a newborn in the house. And second, they'll understand that caring for a child takes energy and stamina – neither of which you would have when you're down with an infection. (If you have only the sniffles and no fever, the parents will probably want you to come to work anyway.)

Hopefully, you'll be able to come up with a backup plan together. Maybe there's a neighbour, relative or friend who can step in to relieve you. Or maybe one of the parents can work from home for the day.

No backup to be found? Dose yourself with some non-drowsy-making medicine to fight those sniffles and soothe that throat, drink plenty of fluids (which will help you feel better faster) and remember to keep your germs to yourself by washing your hands often, turning or covering your mouth with a tissue when you cough and sneeze, and avoiding close cuddles and kisses.

STAYING HEALTHY

Q *'Do I have to worry about catching something from the kids I take care of?'*

A An ounce of protection is worth more than a pound of cure. So protect yourself. If you didn't have all your immunizations as a child (or you're not sure what you've had), it's a good idea to visit a doctor before you begin working with kids. As for avoiding sniffles and the flu: if you're healthy, eat right and wash your hands often (plus, no nibbling on those sickbed leftovers!), you can treat a sick child without getting sick yourself.

TRICKS OF THE TRADE

happy hand washing

Kids are famous for the two-second hand wash. (Half the time, their hands don't even get wet!) To make hand washing fun – and more effective – have the child sing 'Happy Birthday' (or another favourite tune) three times. Once the song's over, she can stop washing.

CHILDPROOF YOURSELF

To keep a child really safe you'll have to 'childproof' yourself. Keep these tips in mind:

■ Know where the first-aid supplies and emergency numbers are kept.

■ Don't carry hot food or drink and a baby at the same time.

■ Don't hold a baby while cooking at the stove. A sudden jump or squirm could lead to a burn. Also, don't leave a cup of coffee or bowl of soup anywhere near baby's reach.

■ When cooking, make sure all the pot and pan handles face away from the edge of the stove, so baby can't pull them down. Keep the dishwasher closed.

■ Don't place baby on a countertop. Babies can fall off easily, and their curiosity can lead them to touch harmful things.

■ Clear the floor of papers, toys or anything that can trip up a little cruiser. Wipe up any spills on slippery floors.

■ When cleaning, don't leave cleaning fluids or detergents around, keep vacuum cords out of reach (and unplugged) and never leave a filled bucket when a baby is near (children can fall in and drown in only a few inches of water).

■ Keep the bathroom door (and the door to any dangerous room) closed and preferably latched.

■ Always supervise young children. Never leave a young child home alone. A child under five should not be left alone for even a moment while you run out to get the post. A child should never be left alone in a car.

■ Keep the door locked when you're in the home and ask who's there before opening the door. If it's a service person, ask to see identification before you unlock the door. If the parents have not told you to expect a repairman, call them before you let the person in.

■ Don't give out private information over the phone. If someone calls for the parents when they're not home, take a message, but do not give out work or mobile phone numbers unless you've been told to do so.

our children, our home

Childcare providers need to have all the essential information about a child or children (and a home and house rules) at her fingertips. That's what this chapter is about. Parents should fill out the following pages (writing in pencil, so they can easily make changes as their children grow). Nannies and babysitters should refer to it often. Of course, not all sections apply to all children.

keeping children safe

The first-aid supplies are located _____

The emergency numbers are posted _____

The best escape route out of the home is _____

The fire extinguisher is located _____

If you smell gas _____

If a pipe bursts or there's a water leak _____

If there's a powercut _____

Torches are located _____

If there's a local or national emergency _____

Other instructions: _____

_____

_____

common illnesses

COLD OR FLU

Special foods: _____

Special drinks: _____

Special medications: _____

Call the parents if _____

Other instructions: _____

_____

DIARRHOEA OR VOMITING

Special foods: _____

Special drinks: _____

Special medications: _____

Call the parents if _____

Other instructions: _____

_____

FEVER

Take the child's temperature when _____

_____

Use this type of thermometer: _____

Call the parents if _____

Other instructions: _____

_____

MEDICATION FOR PAIN OR FEVER

Use only the following pain-relieving and fever-reducing medicines:

_____

Child: _____ Dose to be given: _____

Child: _____ Dose to be given: _____

Child: _____ Dose to be given: _____

If parents can't be reached and the child needs pain-relieving or
fever-reducing medicine, you should _____

_____

_____

The following nonmedicinal remedies can be used: _____

_____

Other instructions: _____

_____

_____

regular medications

Child: _____

Medication _____

Dose _____ Time _____

Child: _____

Medication _____

Dose _____ Time _____

Child: _____

Medication _____

Dose _____ Time _____

feeding the baby

BREAST MILK

Feed the baby: ❑ ON DEMAND ❑ ON SCHEDULE

If on schedule, feed the baby at these times: _____

Amount the baby receives at each feeding: _____

Stored breast milk is kept in the _____

Warm the bottle? ❑ YES ❑ NO

If you run out of breast milk during the day _____

Give the last bottle feeding of the day at this time: _____

Other instructions: _____

_____

FORMULA

Feed the baby: ❑ ON DEMAND ❑ ON SCHEDULE

Feed the baby at these times: _____

The baby drinks this amount of formula at each feeding: _____

Use this type of formula: _____

Formula is kept in the _____

Special water preparation instructions (boil first, use tap, use bottled

water): _____

_____

Warm the bottle? ❑ YES ❑ NO

Other instructions: _____

_____

Special bottle-sterilizing instructions: _____

Does the baby drink water? ❑ YES ❑ NO

SOLID FOOD

The baby eats: ❑ STORE-BOUGHT BABY FOOD

　　　　　　　❑ HOMEMADE FOOD

Prepare homemade baby food by _____

_____

Feed the baby solids at these times: _____

The baby is allergic to _____

_____

The baby can eat the following foods:

❑ Rice cereal (prepared this way: _____)

❑ Barley cereal (prepared this way: _____)

❑ Oat cereal (prepared this way: _____)

❑ Applesauce

❑ Bananas (prepared this way: _____)

❑ Pears (prepared this way: _____)

❑ Peaches (prepared this way: _____)

❑ Peas (prepared this way: _____)

❑ Carrots (prepared this way: _____)

❑ Green beans (prepared this way: _____)

❑ Sweet potato (prepared this way: _____)

❑ Squash (prepared this way: _____)

❑ Chicken (prepared this way: _____)

❑ Turkey (prepared this way: _____)

❑ Lamb (prepared this way: _____)

❑ Beef (prepared this way: _____)

❑ Avocado (prepared this way: _____)

❑ Egg yolk (prepared this way: _____)

❑ Crackers (that dissolve easily in baby's mouth)

❑ Rice cakes

❑ Yogurt

❑ Cheese

❑ Pasta (prepared this way: _____)

❑ Beans (such as lentils, butter beans, kidney beans, prepared this way:_____)

The baby eats these between-meal snacks: _____

_____

The baby drinks from: ❑ A BOTTLE ❑ A CUP

Other instructions: _____

_____

feeding the toddler or school child

Child: _____

Serve breakfast at this time: _____

    Favourite breakfasts: _____

Serve lunch at this time: _____

    Favourite lunches: _____

Serve snack at this time: _____

    Favourite snacks: _____

Serve dinner at this time: _____

    Favourite dinners: _____

Favourite drink: _____

Favourite cup: _____

Favourite plate/bowl: _____

Foods to avoid: _____

Allergies: _____

    Child should not eat: _____

    Child should not drink: _____

Picky eating habits: _____

Other instructions: _____

_____

Child: _____

Serve breakfast at this time: _____

    Favourite breakfasts: _____

Serve lunch at this time: _____

    Favourite lunches: _____

Serve snack at this time: _____

    Favourite snacks: _____

Serve dinner at this time: _____

    Favourite dinners: _____

Favourite drink: _____

Favourite cup: _____

Favourite plate/bowl: _____

Foods to avoid: _____

Allergies: _____

    Child should not eat: _____

    Child should not drink: _____

Picky eating habits: _____

Other instructions: _____

_____

nappies

Child: _____

Nappy size: _____

Use: ❑ WIPES ❑ WATER AND COTTON BALLS

Use this nappy ointment/cream: _____

How to treat nappy rash: _____

_____

Other instructions: _____

_____

Child: _____

Nappy size: _____

Use: ❑ WIPES ❑ WATER AND COTTON BALLS

Use this nappy ointment/cream: _____

How to treat nappy rash: _____

_____

Other instructions: _____

_____

playing with the baby

The baby likes to play these games and with these toys:

_____

_____

_____

Places to go where baby can practise crawling or walking: _____
_____

The baby's favourite songs and rhymes are: _____
_____
_____

The baby's favourite books are: _____
_____
_____

Other playing guidelines: _____
_____
_____

playing with the toddler or school child

Child: _____

Favourite games to play: _____
_____

Favourite books to read: _____
_____

Favourite songs to sing: _____
_____

These TV shows are okay to watch: _____
_____
_____

Limit TV watching to (minutes/hours): _____

No TV watching at these times: _____

The child can watch the following videos: _____

_____

_____

The child can spend this much time on the computer each day

(or each week): _____

The following CD-ROMs are acceptable: _____

_____

_____

Internet guidelines: _____

_____

_____

Playing with friends guidelines: _____

_____

_____

Other playing guidelines: _____

_____

_____

Child: _____

Favourite games to play: _____

_____

Favourite books to read: _____

_____

Favourite songs to sing: _____

_____

These TV shows are okay to watch: _____

_____

_____

Limit TV watching to (minutes/hours): _____

No TV watching at these times: _____

The child can watch the following videos: _____

_____

_____

The child can spend this much time on the computer each day

(or each week): _____

The following CD-ROMs are acceptable: _____

_____

_____

Internet guidelines: _____

_____

_____

Playing with friends guidelines: _____

_____

_____

Other playing guidelines: _____

_____

_____

Child: _____

Favourite games to play: _____

_____

Favourite books to read: _____

_____

Favourite songs to sing: _____

_____

These TV shows are okay to watch: _____

_____

_____

Limit TV watching to (minutes/hours): _____

No TV watching at these times: _____

The child can watch the following videos: _____

_____

_____

The child can spend this much time on the computer each day

(or each week): _____

The following CD-ROMs are acceptable: _____

_____

_____

Internet guidelines: _____

_____

_____

Playing with friends guidelines: _____

_____

_____

Other playing guidelines: _____

_____

_____

going out

Child: _____

In hot weather, dress the child in _____

_____

In cold weather, dress the child in _____

_____

Good toys to take along: _____

_____

Don't forget to always bring _____

_____

The best playgrounds to visit are _____

_____

The child likes to use this equipment at the playground: _____

_____

Use this sunscreen: _____

Car safety rules: _____

_____

_____

Follow these additional outdoor safety rules: _____

_____

_____

Other instructions: _____

_____

_____

_____

Child: _____

In hot weather, dress the child in _____

_____

In cold weather, dress the child in _____

_____

Good toys to take along: _____

_____

Don't forget to always bring _____

_____

The best playgrounds to visit are _____

_____

The child likes to use this equipment at the playground: _____

_____

Use this sunscreen: _____

Car safety rules: _____

_____

_____

Follow these additional outdoor safety rules: _____

_____

_____

Other instructions: _____

_____

_____

_____

bathing

The baby should be bathed this often: _____

Children should be bathed this often: _____

Shampooed this often: _____

Give the bath at this time: _____

Children like to play with these toys in the bath: _____

_____

Special bath instructions for the baby: _____

_____

Special bath instructions for other children: _____

_____

sleeping

BABY

The baby's nap schedule: _____

The baby's bedtime is _____

The baby's bedtime or naptime routine: _____

_____

Does the baby like to be swaddled: ❑ YES ❑ NO

The baby likes to fall asleep this way: _____

_____

If the baby cries when it's time for a nap or bed _____

_____

If the baby wakes up during the night or during a nap _____

_____

Other instructions: _____

_____

_____

TODDLER/SCHOOL CHILD

Child: _____

Child takes _____ naps at these times: _____

Child's naptime routine is _____

_____

Napping guidelines: _____

Bedtime is _____

Bedtime routines: _____

_____

Suggestions for getting the child to sleep: _____

_____

If the child won't stay in bed _____

The bedroom door should be: ❏ OPEN ❏ SHUT

The bedroom light should be: ❏ ON ❏ OFF

Other instructions: _____

_____

_____

Child: _____

Child takes _____ naps at these times: _____

Child's naptime routine is _____

_____

Napping guidelines: _____

Bedtime is _____

Bedtime routines: _____

_____

Suggestions for getting the child to sleep: _____

_____

If the child won't stay in bed _____

The bedroom door should be: ❑ OPEN   ❑ SHUT

The bedroom light should be: ❑ ON   ❑ OFF

Other instructions: _____

_____

_____

comfort objects

BABY

These comfort objects are okay: _____

Limits on comfort objects: _____

TODDLER/SCHOOL CHILD

Child: _____

These comfort objects are okay: _____

Limits on comfort objects: _____

_____

Child: _____

These comfort objects are okay: _____

Limits on comfort objects: _____

_____

behaviour & discipline

BABY

The best way to calm the baby when crying: _____

_____

_____

The baby uses this comfort item to calm down (dummy, swaddling, fingers): _____

_____

The baby's favourite calming tune(s): _____

_____

Use massage? ❑ YES ❑ NO

The baby likes to be massaged like this: _____

_____

   Best time for massage: _____

Tips to ease separation anxiety: _____

_____

The baby is frightened by _____

_____

Ease the baby's fears by _____

Other instructions: _____

_____

TODDLER/SCHOOL CHILD

Child: _____

Ways to calm child down: _____

_____

Ways to tame a tantrum: _____

_____

Important routines: _____

_____

Manners that are important to teach and tips for teaching them:

_____

_____

Ways to help with transitions: _____

_____

Acceptable types of discipline: _____

_____

_____

Time-out should last _____

Where time-out should be given: _____

During the time-out, the child can _____

_____

Time-outs should be given for these kinds of behaviour: _____

_____

_____

Keep these guidelines in mind when giving a time-out: _____

_____

_____

Don't use these forms of discipline: _____

_____

Other instructions: _____

_____

Child: _____

Ways to calm child down: _____

_____

Ways to tame a tantrum: _____

_____

Important routines: _____

_____

Manners that are important to teach and tips for teaching them:

_____

_____

Ways to help with transitions: _____

_____

Acceptable types of discipline: _____

_____

_____

Time-out should last _____

Where time-out should be given: _____

During the time-out, the child can _____

_____

Time-outs should be given for these kinds of behaviour: _____

_____

_____

Keep these guidelines in mind when giving a time-out: _____

_____

_____

Don't use these forms of discipline: _____

_____

Other instructions: _____

_____

Child: _____

Ways to calm child down: _____

_____

Ways to tame a tantrum: _____

_____

Important routines: _____

_____

Manners that are important to teach and tips for teaching them:

_____

_____

Ways to help with transitions: _____

_____

Acceptable types of discipline: _____

_____

_____

Time-out should last _____

Where time-out should be given: _____

During the time-out, the child can _____

_____

Time-outs should be given for these kinds of behaviour: _____

_____

_____

Keep these guidelines in mind when giving a time-out: _____

_____

_____

Don't use these forms of discipline: _____

_____

Other instructions: _____

_____

child's responsibilities

Child: _____

The child is responsible for these chores: _____

_____

If the child doesn't do chores _____

_____

The child can do these things by him/herself:

❏ TOY CLEANUP ❏ CLEARING DISHES ❏ GETTING DRESSED

❏ PICKING OUT CLOTHES ❏ BRUSHING TEETH ❏ OTHER

Child: _____

The child is responsible for these chores: _____

_____

If the child doesn't do chores _____

_____

The child can do these things by him/herself:

❑ TOY CLEANUP   ❑ CLEARING DISHES   ❑ GETTING DRESSED

❑ PICKING OUT CLOTHES   ❑ BRUSHING TEETH   ❑ OTHER

Child: _____

The child is responsible for these chores: _____

_____

If the child doesn't do chores _____

_____

The child can do these things by him/herself:

❑ TOY CLEANUP   ❑ CLEARING DISHES   ❑ GETTING DRESSED

❑ PICKING OUT CLOTHES   ❑ BRUSHING TEETH   ❑ OTHER

the special things

Child: _____

Special likes and dislikes: _____

_____

Special talents: _____

The child loves _____

_____

The child responds best to _____

_____

Child: _____
Special likes and dislikes: _____

_____

Special talents: _____
The child loves _____
The child responds best to _____

_____

Child: _____
Special likes and dislikes: _____

_____

Special talents: _____
The child loves _____

_____

The child responds best to _____

_____

siblings

Privacy rules: _____

_____

_____

What to do if children are fighting: _____

_____

_____

Tips for twins: _____

_____

_____

Other instructions: _____

_____

potty

Child: _____

Special potty or toilet instructions: _____

_____

The child uses: ❏ POTTY CHAIR ❏ POTTY SEAT ❏ TOILET

During the day, the child uses:

❏ NAPPIES ❏ PULL-UPS ❏ TRAINING PANTS ❏ PANTS/KNICKERS

At naptime, the child uses:

❏ NAPPIES ❏ PULL-UPS ❏ TRAINING PANTS ❏ PANTS/KNICKERS

At night, the child uses:

❏ NAPPIES ❏ PULL-UPS ❏ TRAINING PANTS ❏ PANTS/KNICKERS

During potty training, use these tricks: _____

_____

_____

The child usually has a b.m. at these times: ____

The child needs to be reminded to go: ❏ YES ❏ NO

In case of a potty accident: _____

_____

Other instructions: _____

_____

_____

Child: _____

Special potty or toilet instructions: _____

_____

The child uses: ❑ POTTY CHAIR   ❑ POTTY SEAT   ❑ TOILET

During the day, the child uses:

❑ NAPPIES   ❑ PULL-UPS   ❑ TRAINING PANTS   ❑ PANTS/KNICKERS

At naptime, the child uses:

❑ NAPPIES   ❑ PULL-UPS   ❑ TRAINING PANTS   ❑ PANTS/KNICKERS

At night, the child uses:

❑ NAPPIES   ❑ PULL-UPS   ❑ TRAINING PANTS   ❑ PANTS/KNICKERS

During potty training, use these tricks: _____

_____

_____

The child usually has a b.m. at these times: _____

The child needs to be reminded to go: ❑ YES   ❑ NO

In case of a potty accident: _____

_____

Other instructions: _____

_____

_____

Child: _____

Special potty or toilet instructions: _____

_____

The child uses: ❑ POTTY CHAIR   ❑ POTTY SEAT   ❑ TOILET

During the day, the child uses:

❑ NAPPIES   ❑ PULL-UPS   ❑ TRAINING PANTS   ❑ PANTS/KNICKERS

At naptime, the child uses:

❑ NAPPIES   ❑ PULL-UPS   ❑ TRAINING PANTS   ❑ PANTS/KNICKERS

At night, the child uses:

❑ NAPPIES   ❑ PULL-UPS   ❑ TRAINING PANTS   ❑ PANTS/KNICKERS

During potty training, use these tricks: _____

_____

_____

The child usually has a b.m. at these times: _____

The child needs to be reminded to go: ❑ YES   ❑ NO

In case of a potty accident: _____

_____

Other instructions: _____

_____

_____

house rules

Here are some rules we want the children to follow: _____

_____

_____

_____

_____

Phone rules: _____

_____

Car rules and instructions: _____

_____

Visitor rules: _____

_____

Food rules: _____

_____

Pet rules: _____

_____

CHILDCARER'S ADDITIONAL RESPONSIBILITIES:

❑ LAUNDRY ❑ ERRANDS ❑ CLEANING ❑ DRIVING

❑ COOKING ❑ OTHER

Other instructions: _____

_____

_____

_____

activities & after school clubs

MONDAY

Child: _____ Activity: _____

Time: _____ Location: _____

Share driving with: _____ Contact number: _____

Child: _____ Activity: _____

Time: _____ Location: _____

Share driving with: _____ Contact number: _____

TUESDAY

Child: _____ Activity: _____

Time: _____ Location: _____

Share driving with: _____ Contact number: _____

Child: _____ Activity: _____

Time: _____ Location: _____

Share driving with: _____ Contact number: _____

WEDNESDAY

Child: _____ Activity: _____

Time: _____ Location: _____

Share driving with: _____ Contact number: _____

Child: _____ Activity: _____

Time: _____ Location: _____

Share driving with: _____ Contact number: _____

THURSDAY

Child: _____   Activity: _____

Time: _____   Location: _____

Share driving with: _____   Contact number: _____

Child: _____   Activity: _____

Time: _____   Location: _____

Share driving with: _____   Contact number: _____

FRIDAY

Child: _____   Activity: _____

Time: _____   Location: _____

Share driving with: _____   Contact number: _____

Child: _____   Activity: _____

Time: _____   Location: _____

Share driving with: _____   Contact number: _____

SATURDAY

Child: _____   Activity: _____

Time: _____   Location: _____

Share driving with: _____   Contact number: _____

Child: _____   Activity: _____

Time: _____   Location: _____

Share driving with: _____   Contact number: _____

SUNDAY

Child: _____ Activity: _____

Time: _____ Location: _____

Share driving with: _____ Contact number: _____

Child: _____ Activity: _____

Time: _____ Location: _____

Share driving with: _____ Contact number: _____

school

Child: _____

School: _____

Address: _____

Phone: _____

Teacher's name: _____

Days attending school: _____

Drop-off time: _____ Drop-off location: _____

Pickup time: _____ Pickup location: _____

Does child take a bus? ❏ YES ❏ NO

    Bus drop-off time: _____ Drop-off location: _____

    Bus pickup time: _____ Bus pickup location: _____

Pack these lunches for child this way: _____

_____

_____

Pack these: _____

Other school instructions: _____

_____

_____

Child: _____

School: _____

Address: _____

Phone: _____

Teacher's name: _____

Days attending school: _____

Drop-off time: _____ Drop-off location: _____

Pickup time: _____ Pickup location: _____

Does child take a bus? ❑ YES ❑ NO

   Bus drop-off time: _____ Drop-off location: _____

   Bus pickup time: _____ Bus pickup location: _____

Pack these lunches for child this way: _____

_____

_____

Pack these: _____

Other school instructions: _____

_____

_____

Child: _____

School: _____

Address: _____

Phone: _____

Teacher's name: _____

Days attending school: _____

Drop-off time: _____ Drop-off location: _____

Pickup time: _____ Pickup location: _____

Does child take a bus? ❑ YES ❑ NO

   Bus drop-off time: _____ Drop-off location: _____

   Bus pickup time: _____ Bus pickup location: _____

Pack these lunches for child this way: _____

_____

_____

Pack these: _____

Other school instructions: _____

_____

_____

playmates

Child: _____

Friend's name: _____

Parent's name: _____

Childcarer's name: _____

Phone: _____ Address: _____

Friend's name: _____

Parent's name: _____

Childcarer's name: _____

Phone: _____ Address: _____

Friend's name: _____

Parent's name: _____

Childcarer's name: _____

Phone: _____ Address: _____

Friend's name: _____

Parent's name: _____

Childcarer's name:_____

Phone: _____ Address: _____

Child: _____

Friend's name: _____

Parent's name: _____

Childcarer's name:_____

Phone: _____ Address: _____

Friend's name: _____

Parent's name: _____

Childcarer's name:_____

Phone: _____ Address: _____

Friend's name: _____

Parent's name: _____

Childcarer's name:_____

Phone: _____ Address: _____

Friend's name: _____

Parent's name: _____

Childcarer's name:_____

Phone: _____ Address: _____

Child: _____

Friend's name: _____

Parent's name: _____

Childcarer's name:_____

Phone: _____ Address: _____

Friend's name: _____

Parent's name: _____

Childcarer's name:_____

Phone: _____ Address: _____

Friend's name: _____

Parent's name: _____

Childcarer's name:_____

Phone: _____ Address: _____

Friend's name: _____

Parent's name: _____

Childcarer's name:_____

Phone: _____ Address: _____

playgroup

Playgroup meets on:_____

    Time:_____

    Address: _____

    Contact number: _____

Playgroup meets on:_____

    Time:_____

    Address: _____

    Contact number: _____

keeping connected

E-mail addresses: _____

Computer instructions: _____

_____

_____

_____

Keep in touch during the day by _____

_____

Other instructions: _____

_____

_____

_____

index